SHATTERED

SHATTERED

A Memoir

Hanif Kureishi

ecco

An Imprint of HarperCollins*Publishers*

Originally published in the United Kingdom
in 2024 by Hamish Hamilton.

FIRST U.S. EDITION

Library of Congress Cataloging-in-Publication Data
has been applied for.

ISBN 978-0-06-336050-1

24 25 26 27 28 LBC 5 4 3 2 1

For Isabella

This book began as a series of dispatches dictated from my hospital bed in Italy and later in London, after my accident on Boxing Day 2022. My partner, Isabella, and my sons took down my words as the events happened. They have since been revised, expanded and edited by the same method, working with my son Carlo, at my home in West London, where I am now.

THE FALL

On Boxing Day, in Rome, after taking a comfortable walk to the Piazza del Popolo, followed by a stroll through the Villa Borghese, and then back to the apartment, I had a fall.

Sitting at a table in Isabella's living room with my iPad in front of me, I had just seen Mo Salah score against Aston Villa. I was sipping a beer when I began to feel dizzy. I leant forward and put my head between my legs; I woke up a few minutes later in a pool of blood, my neck in a grotesquely twisted position, Isabella on her knees beside me.

I then experienced what can only be described as a scooped, semicircular object with talons scuttling towards me. Using what was left of my reason, I saw this was one of my hands, an uncanny thing over which I had no agency.

It occurred to me that there was no coordination between my mind and what remained of my body. I had become divorced from myself. I believed I was dying, that I had three breaths

3

left. It seemed like a miserable and ignoble way to go.

People say when you're about to die your life passes before your eyes, but for me it wasn't the past but the future that I thought about — everything I was being robbed of, all the things I wanted to do.

GEMELLI HOSPITAL, ROME

Isabella and I live in London but we were staying in her apartment in Rome for Christmas, and it was there that I had my fall, sitting at the large round table, covered in books and papers, where she and I work together in the mornings.

From the bathroom, she heard my frantic shout, came in and called an ambulance. She saved my life and kept me calm, crouching down beside me. I told her I wanted to FaceTime my three sons and say goodbye, but Isabella said it wasn't a good idea, it would frighten and appal them.

For a few days I was profoundly traumatized, altered and unrecognizable to myself.

Now I am in the Gemelli Hospital, Rome. I cannot move my arms and legs. I cannot scratch my nose, make a phone call or feed myself. As you can imagine, this is both humiliating and degrading, making me a burden for others. According to my hospital report, my fall resulted in neck hyperextension and immediate tetraplegia. An MRI scan showed a severe stenosis of the vertebral canal with signs of spinal cord injury from C3 to C5. In layman's terms, the vertebrae at the top of my spine suffered a kind of whiplash. I've had an operation on my neck to relieve compression on my spine where the injury is, and have shown minor motor improvements.

I have sensation and some movement in all my limbs, I did not have what they call a 'complete break'. I will begin physio and rehabilitation as soon as possible.

At the moment, it is unclear whether I will be able to walk again, or if I'll ever be able to hold a pen. I am speaking these words through Isabella, who is slowly typing them into her iPad. I am determined to keep writing, it has never mattered to me more.

06/01/2023

I wasn't a happy child but I wasn't an unhappy one either. Once I could read I was free. I could go to libraries every day, often accompanied by my mother, and I saw that books were a way out of my immediate surroundings.

Soon I learned to cycle. Alone, I could explore the streets and fields of the countrified semi-suburbs in which I grew up. It was a county called Kent, which had been bombed to hell not long before I was born.

In those days parents were less police-like. They gave you a penny at the beginning of the day and didn't expect to see you until the evening. I cycled all day, stopped where I wanted and talked to anyone who had a story for me. I am still like that.

The third element in my liberation was the discovery of my father's typing manual. My father himself had been a journalist and was writing fiction. His vigorous typing in his sexy shirtsleeves seemed impressive.

One day he bought a little portable typewriter in a blue case of which he was incredibly proud. He swung it round and round, because it was light, and suddenly announced he was going to Vietnam to be a war correspondent like Hemingway or Norman Mailer.

I started to blindfold myself with my school tie and found I could type the correct words in order without looking.

It was exhilarating. I had been reading *Crime and Punishment* at the time, always a cheery go-to book for a young man, and as practice I began to copy out pages from this great novel.

At school I had been a disaster, but at last I had found something I could do. I never had the desire to write underwater stories, adventure stories or amazing tales involving giants, dwarfs, elves or mermaids.

I didn't know much about those things, but I did know the people around me. And I guess that made me into something of a realist. One day, looking out of the window at school, I called myself a writer.

I found the title suited me like a good shirt.

I was keen for others to apply the word to me even though I hadn't yet written anything.

After all, at school many words had already been applied to me, words like 'Brownie', or 'Paki', or 'Shit-face', so I found my own word, I stuck to it, and never let it go. It is still my word.

Excuse me for a moment, I must have an enema now.

The last time a medical digit entered my backside was a few years ago. As the nurse flipped me over she asked, 'How long did it take you to write *Midnight's Children*?' I replied, 'If I had indeed written that, don't you think I would have gone private?'

07/01/2023

Before my accident, when I woke up in the morning, the first thing I would do is make my coffee and go upstairs to my desk, which overlooks the street. Around the edge of the desk, in various pots and old coffee cups, I have dozens of fountain pens, pencils, markers; I also have many bottles of ink, in numerous colours, from the ludicrous to the sober.

I would pick up a pen and make a mark on a page of good thick paper, then make another mark, write a word, a sentence and another sentence, until I felt something waking up inside me. The writing zigzagged across the page in multicolours, as though there had been an accident in a schoolroom.

As I made these marks, I began to hear characters speaking; if I was lucky they might start talking to each other, or even amusing one another. I would feel excited and that my life had meaning at last.

I'm sure painters, architects and gardeners

love their tools, and see them as an extension of their body. I hope one day I will be able to go back to using my own precious and beloved instruments.

Excuse me, I'm being injected in my belly with something called Heparina, a blood thinner.

I find that writing by hand, moving my wrist across the page – the feeling of skin on paper – is more like drawing than typing. I wouldn't want to write directly into a machine, it's too formal.

After a while, one word will push out another word, followed by another word, and more words and sentences may follow. I sit at my desk in my swirly Paul Smith pyjamas, and after an hour something I can use may have emerged.

When I read it through, something usually attracts my attention, which I can develop. I guess this method is now known as free writing or free association. You start with nothing and after some time you find yourself in a new place.

My hands continue to feel like alien objects. They're swollen, I cannot open or close them, and when they are under the sheets, I could not tell you where they are precisely. They may in fact be in another building altogether, having a drink with friends.

I have been moved from the ICU to a small grim side room. There is a picture of the Virgin Mary ahead of me, and the view outside the window, which I cannot see myself, is of a car park, motorway, and Roman pine trees, which look like parasols. I tell Isabella the place hasn't been decorated since Hemingway left.

I was low yesterday. Trying to dictate these words to Isabella, I became impatient with the slowness of the process. She is Italian and English is her second language, so she doesn't always get what I say.

Carlo Kureishi, the second of my twin sons, has now flown out to Italy, and is helping me with this dictation. He is in his late twenties and, like me, read philosophy at university. He enjoys movies and sport and is starting to make his way as a screenwriter. What I like about him is that he can type quickly. Normally, of course, I can write this stuff up myself. I can even spell.

Isabella and I have started to argue. She is in the hospital with me all day, and is looking tired and thin, as she would in the circumstance of this terrible strain. When she turned to me and asked, 'Would you have ever done this for me?' I couldn't answer. I don't know.

Our relationship has taken a new turn, not one we could have anticipated, and we will have to find a new way of loving each other. At the moment, I have no idea how to do this.

A few months ago, Apple Music, on behalf of the Beatles, asked me to write an introduction to their book *Get Back*, to coincide with the release of Peter Jackson's Beatles series on Disney. For a long time I was stumped. What more could there be to say about the Beatles?

And then it occurred to me that those four boys, with their numerous collaborators, were able to do things together that they couldn't do apart. This is both a miracle and a terrible dependency. In my experience, all artists are collaborationists.

If you are not collaborating with a particular individual, you are collaborating with the history of the medium, and you're also collaborating with the time, politics and culture within which you exist. There are no individuals.

In this somewhat desolate Roman hospital, in a suburb of Rome, I am writing these words to try to reach someone, and I am, at the same time, attempting to connect with Isabella, to make a new relationship out of an old one. You'd think I'd have enough on my plate.

I wish what had happened to me had never happened, but there isn't a family on the planet that will evade catastrophe or disaster. But out of these unexpected breaks, there must be new opportunities for creativity.

If you were with me tonight, my reader, we would each pour a large vodka with a juicy mixer and drink and embrace each other with a little hope.

08/01/2023

I sat up today.

I sat up today after eight days on my back.

Four physiotherapists came to my room. They started to move me with the determination of sitting me up. They turned me, and for a moment I sat on the bed, with my feet on the floor, staring ahead of me. I have to say, I felt proud and amazed and incredibly dizzy.

When I first came to London to work in the theatre, I was a stage manager on a magnificent production of Kafka's the *Metamorphosis*. Every night, seeing the actor trying to untangle himself from his new spiky black limbs, was like witnessing a macabre dance. Little did I know, years later, sitting up straight on the edge of a bed, I would undergo my own metamorphosis.

I feel crumpled and uneven. I slump. I used to choose my shirts carefully, in colours I thought suited me. I moved lightly as I swung around my city. Now I can't even do up my own buttons.

The word 'vocation' comes from the Latin *vocatio*, 'a call, summons'. Here in hospital, where I spend nights and days with nurses and doctors, the word has gained resonance for me. Like many artists, I don't consider my work as a pastime or a job, but a form of integration into the world of others.

Sometimes at three or four in the morning, when I am my most sleepless, a charming young man comes and sits with me. He wears glasses and a face mask, and I doubt I'd ever recognize him on the street. Apparently, he is a highly trained pianist as well as a doctor.

He asks me whether he should become a professional pianist, or remain as a medical practitioner. This is a question I cannot answer, but since I have nothing but time available to me, it's something I can help him explore.

There are many interpreters of the classical repertoire, but for me, as an artist, one should try to create new things every day, things one has never done before.

So I said to him, in the morning when he is

practising, he should try to create a new sound, one which came from himself.

This can be frightening, but fear is the engine of art. You may be afraid of presenting something personal to the world, but you can never anticipate how the other will receive it.

From what I could see of his face, he looked a bit anxious, and I wondered whether I had given him something, after all he had given me as a doctor.

I grew up in a mixed British-Indian household, and as a child I spent a lot of time listening to people speaking in a language I didn't understand: Urdu or Punjabi, mixed with cockney English. Not understanding Italian is frustrating, but I try to ask simple and straightforward questions like, 'When did you know you wanted to be a nurse or a doctor?' or 'When was the moment you realized you'd fallen in love?'

I find in these trying circumstances that the naive questions are the ones that cut through. I asked one nurse how she found her vocation. She said, when she was seven years old, a nurse came to the house and saved her mother, and at that moment, the girl realized she had to work in medicine.

I decided to become a writer when I was fourteen or fifteen years old. I never thought I'd be good at anything else, and sometimes I wonder whether having chosen so early excluded me from too many other things.

I could perhaps have become a barber, an architect, or Chancellor of the Exchequer. But a writer I am, and sitting here again in this dreary room for another week, like a Beckettian chattering mouth, all I can do is speak, but I can also listen.

I can wiggle my toes and move my feet up and down. My left foot is stronger than my right, from which there is less response. I can straighten and bend my left leg, but there is minimal movement in my right. I can move my arse and even jerk it about. As for the surface of my skin, I am a little numb below the waist, but I have sensibility all the way down. I am not in a neck brace and do not have the petrified look paralysed people can have. I am able to move my neck and shoulders, and can move my right arm and hold up my right hand a little, but it is weak at the wrist and hangs limply down. I can't close or open my fingers. My hands are inert, stiff and swollen, and they could just as well belong to someone else. I can move my left arm, but it is slightly dislocated and painful. There is not much range. The fingers on my left hand are hyperextended and I can move them a little. Again, I cannot grip anything with them. As far as I can tell, my brain is unaffected, and I can think as I did before.

Two of my sons, Kier and Sachin, have come to Rome and seen me for the first time in this state. Kier teaches piano and guitar; he's skinny, fair-skinned and with blue eyes. Sachin is darker and muscular, and writes on a TV soap opera. They were shocked, we all cried a little, but they tried to remain upbeat and humorous. No one knows whether or how I will progress, so it is difficult to predict what the future will look like for us as a family.

I wouldn't advise having an accident like mine, but I would say that lying completely inert and silent in a drab room on the outskirts of Rome, without much distraction, is certainly good for creativity. Deprived of newspapers, music, and all the rest of it, you will find yourself becoming imaginative.

Recently, in my late sixties, I had felt myself slowing down as a writer, but the ideas have not stopped coming. Characters, voices, situations – I'm as full of them as ever, if not more. So a break of a few days, with absolutely nothing in your life to distract you, might be a good form of shock therapy for a stuck writer. In fact, there probably are no stuck writers, just resting ones, and those who wait.

My friend Salman Rushdie, one of the bravest men I know, who has stood up to the most violent form of Islamofascism, writes to me every single day, encouraging patience. He should know. He gives me courage.

Since I began writing these pieces, numerous articles regarding me and my work have appeared in the world's press. It has been gratifying since they are mostly complimentary. It is a bit like experiencing the press coverage you might receive had you died, to have your work and place as an artist addressed and reconsidered. It is both moving and uncanny.

The only good thing to be said for paralysis is that you don't have to move to shit and piss.

09/01/2023

Since I became a vegetable I have never been so busy. Last night at around nine I watched a few minutes of a film, which I enjoyed. Then I lost connection and everything went dark.

I fell asleep and woke at one and was conscious for the rest of the night. I had many ideas but since I can't use my hands and make notes, I have to remember them until the next day when I can shout them at Carlo down the phone.

This is how I write these days; I fling a net over more or less random thoughts, draw it in and hope some kind of pattern emerges.

This morning three very beautiful Italian physiotherapists came to my room. They wore clean white uniforms with orange trim. They put me in a blue plastic sling, hoisted me up and dropped me into a wheelchair. I was turned around and for the first time I was able to see the other side of my room. I saw the Italian sky through the window, some trees and a cloud and a few birds. I believed that things might begin to improve.

My heart is like a singing bird.

The physios left and another came in. A gentle man, handsome, who also works for Roma football club. He had been inspecting Tammy Abraham's legs before examining mine.

He caressed my fingers and my feet; he opened my hands and pulsated them delicately. I began to feel that I had a whole body, not just a patchwork of random pieces thrown together as if by Mary Shelley's imagination.

Still, I have lost all sense of time. I don't know what day it is or even what month.

I have become a big admirer of Italian men. I find them good-looking. Their skin is smooth and it glows. Their sharp dark body hair is inspiring. They are neither macho nor mummy's boys.

Since I lost my body, to look at, to smell and contemplate the bodies of others in such detail has become an aesthetic pleasure for me. The women too, of course, with their long black hair and glorious eyes.

I've had many intimate conversations with young queer and non-binary staff members. They are afraid for the future of Italy, which has the misfortune of being governed by a fascist.

For these fabulous young people, to make a life they will have to leave their beautiful country and find a more sympathetic and humane environment. This is a great loss.

Italy is one of the great gay civilizations of Europe. The Vatican is gay, as is the fashion industry. The entire aesthetic of the Renaissance is based on polyamorous sexuality.

A few years ago, Britain had a dangerous, if not catastrophic, Brexit debate which tore our country apart. Something similar has happened in Italy with Giorgia Meloni.

All Nazi and fascist programmes believe that the removal of a few miscreants will create a bright and new future. It is a cretinous conviction.

I've enjoyed being in this hospital. Everyone here has treated me with respect and courtesy. But there is something tragic, if not disconcerting, to see how closed off it is when it comes to race. Every day I wonder where my brothers and sisters of colour are.

Are they kept in a special place to avoid contaminating the others? It would be a terrible thing if the country with the best food and culture and the most cultivated people turned itself into an island, isolated from the rest of the world.

Isabella d'Amico wants to make an intervention here. She says my knowledge of her country is not so varied and wise, and that I am not best placed to comment on the ills of Italian society given I have not bothered to learn her language. I tell her it would be easier for everyone in Italy to learn English than for me to understand Italian.

Literature, to its glory, is a dirty-bastard form. From the most vulgar and scurrilous, to the most sublime and poetic – you can put anything in a book, twist it about and turn it into something unforgettable. An insect, a hero, a ghost or Frankenstein's monster. Out of these mixings will come impressive horrors and amazements.

Every day when I dictate these thoughts, I open what is left of my broken body to give form to this chaos I have fallen into, to stop myself from dying inside.

10/01/2023

Another shitty night. One of the worst. I went to sleep at eight o'clock after taking my medication and by one o'clock I was wide awake. Not only that, my head became jammed down the side of the bed. I can't move my arms or legs and no one could hear me. It seemed like a good opportunity for some contemplation.

What could I think about?

My father had been a journalist and a writer. Several of my uncles had been journalists in India, running movie or what were called filmie magazines.

I read dozens of biographies of writers when I was a teenager. From Balzac to Proust and Zola, Dickens and Colette and Henry Miller, and the autobiographical masterpieces of my then hero James Baldwin. Their lives, with all the carousing, fucking and fighting and general riotous living, seemed like something to aspire to. When I first began to write, as a disturbed and semi-delinquent teenager, I believed there were people outside my bedroom and the suburbs — at least one person — who would recognize or understand me.

The first writers I met were Brian Patten and Roger McGough, known as the Liverpool poets. As president of the student union at Bromley College of Technology, I organized a gig headlined by the Pink Fairies. Brian Patten was there, a writer published by Penguin. I handed him a brown envelope with ninety pounds in it. He read a poem and then fucked off home on the bus.

When I was twenty-one, I took the train from Bromley South station up to Victoria, walked to Sloane Square, went into the upstairs bar of the Royal Court Theatre and through into the auditorium. Standing onstage was a tall, thin man pointing vigorously at an actress. This was Samuel Beckett in the mid-1970s directing Billie Whitelaw in his play *Footfalls*.

I started to work as an usher at the Royal Court that night and I saw many real writers up close for the first time. I stood within a few feet of the great David Storey, Edward Bond and the masterful Caryl Churchill, who would whizz around the building encouraging the young people.

To me these were astonishing figures because they were capable of making language sing and turning actors into their instruments. I was able to be with people who took the arts seriously, devoting their lives to it.

They were eccentric, mad and serious, passionate about what they did, and they argued furiously among themselves.

Every night I went into the bar next to the Royal Court and sat there with my newspaper. I would stare at Samuel Beckett, a man who liked a drink. I became friends with his brilliant lighting director, Duncan Scott, which enabled me to get closer to Beckett. Contrary to popular belief, he wasn't a miserable git. If a young woman approached him with a pile of his books, Sam would look cheerful and sign them gladly.

Of the young writers, the most charming was always Christopher Hampton, who had a play produced at the Royal Court when he was twenty-one years old, called *Total Eclipse*, about the relationship between Rimbaud and Paul Verlaine. Christopher was gracious enough to introduce me to his agent, Peggy Ramsay, who invited me to her office in the West End.

She was fierce and intimidating and certainly scared the shit out of me. She sat on the couch, waved her legs about and said, 'In my younger days I was never averse to a little fucking in the afternoon.'

I handed her an adaptation I had done of Dostoevsky's *Notes from Underground*. I noticed that somehow she contrived to get strawberry jam on the manuscript, sticking the pages together. With some contempt she handed it back and remarked that it looked a little short.

Many years later, when she had dementia, her office burned down. She told the actor Simon Callow that it was an act of revenge and that I was responsible.

The reason I'm telling you this is not because my head is still stuck between the wall and the bed, and you and I must pass the time with some amusement, but because I need you to know that writers were living and breathing creatures in the world, and were paid to use their imagination.

The second important event in my early writing life was in 1981. I was working in the bookshop at Riverside Studios arts centre in Hammersmith. One evening the guest of honour was Italo Calvino, introduced by Salman Rushdie, whom I met for the first time. After the reading, there was a dinner given by Gaia Servadio in Chelsea (her beautiful daughter, Allegra Mostyn-Owen, later married Boris Johnson).

Salman Rushdie gave me a copy of *Midnight's Children* and I returned to my tiny flat at 48 Barons Court Road, lay on my mattress on the floor and read the book all the way through. I then walked down the river to Hammersmith, up to Chiswick Bridge, and back home. I drank a bottle of wine and read the whole book again.

Rushdie invited me to his house for dinner with Angela Carter. He was a whirl of information, wit and wide talk. He had extensive knowledge, everything from *Star Trek* to the great myths.

Seeing this phenomenon, I realized I had to start over as a person and as a writer. I had to become a comic writer, a writer who could integrate the wildest and the most interesting elements on the same page. It was around this time that I began to take myself seriously, and work longer hours.

The nurse has arrived. She has managed to prise my head from the breech position and settled me down. There is a beautiful opening line in 'Viewfinder', from Raymond Carver's *What We Talk About When We Talk About Love*, which reads: 'A man without hands came to the door to sell me a photograph of my house. Except for the chrome hooks, he was an ordinary-looking man of fifty or so.'

This image struck me tonight, since I am the man with no hands.

11/01/2023

At last, not such a bad night. Asleep at nine and, excluding a few interruptions, I was unconscious until five. The previous evening I had asked for more sleeping aids but was told they had run out. Perhaps I had already consumed the hospital's supply. But last night was better.

Having not left this room for nine days I seem to be adjusting to my condition, unfortunately.

At six thirty in the morning, to the sound of crashing buckets and loud voices, the nurses came to wash and change me. They lift you up in a blanket, roll you around and scrub you. They wash your genitals and your arse, often while singing jolly Italian songs.

One of the male nurses is particularly fond of Bruce Springsteen, and during the procedure he likes to sing along to 'Dancing in the Dark'. I don't mind so much, I enjoy the company.

Next up is breakfast, a bowl of dirty cold tea in which a sugary biscuit is dumped. They spoon it into my mouth.

It's then my physios come. There are four of them. They are determined to get me upright. This involves strapping me into a blue sling with my feet on the floor and standing me up vertically. I have to say this is a horrible experience since I have not been upright for some time.

The world seems at the wrong angle, everything in the incorrect place and the colours flying around, unattached to specific objects, like hallucinations.

I couldn't breathe and thought I might vomit. They laid me down again and said it would take some time to get used to standing up.

My next adventure involves being placed on a trolley and dragged on my back for miles around the hospital for various tests. I begin to figure out where I am from the position of the ceiling tiles.

Two weeks ago a bomb went off in my life which has also shattered the lives of those around me. My partner, my children, my friends. All my relationships are being renegotiated. It makes everybody a little crazy, it changes everything. There is guilt and rage, and people resent their dependence on one another and the fact they can't do everything for themselves. My accident was a physical tragedy, but the emotional outcomes for all of us are going to be significant. I'm proud to be dependent on others who love me. And so far they appear to want to come to my aid. I've had lots of kind offers from friends and strangers suggesting expensive and useful things to help me continue writing. It should go without saying that I am profoundly moved and grateful.

I'd like to add that I really enjoy writing these dispatches from my bed. At least I haven't lost the one thing that was most valuable to me, which is my ability to express myself.

Since I've been here, I've barely moved at all. Carlo started to stretch my limbs a little, raising my arms above my head, applying resistance, and driving my legs up towards my chest. This was the first time I felt like I was in my body since my accident.

Last night things got tense in this little room; Isabella was tired, if not exhausted, and there were some nasty conflicts between us. The issue of the cleaning of my teeth brought things to a head.

Isabella, as you might imagine, is not a dentist. Using a toothbrush, some floss and a cocktail stick, she tried to clean my mouth as I was trying to dictate. I began to feel that I was both a helpless baby and a terrible tyrant; to be in a position like this is to have to endure vulnerability and frustration.

12/01/2023

Last night, Isabella set up a film for me on my iPad before she left. I felt relaxed and was enjoying the movie when the cleaner came in, moved some things around and knocked the iPad on its back. She turned the light off and shut the door behind her.

I was in almost complete darkness. I could still hear the film, however, and tried to work out what was happening from the silhouettes flickering on the ceiling, like a shadow puppet show.

Sometime later I drifted into sleep and started to dream of my hands, which were tied together with a silver cord so I was unable to move them.

For some reason I can't explain, I also had a memory of being on the jury of the Cannes Film Festival in 2009 when Isabelle Huppert was the president.

We jury members, who included Asia Argento and Robin Wright, used to sneak into films early in the morning to avoid the red-carpet exhibition in the evening. It also meant we could leave early if the films were unpleasant, which they often were.

But one film in particular stayed with me. It was Lars von Trier's *Antichrist*, images from which pursued me last night. The best film from that year was Jacques Audiard's *A Prophet*, which surely deserved to win first prize.

I woke up and started to cry. When you cry you must wipe away your tears, which is something I'm unable to do. So my eyes filled with bitter salty water and I got into a panic and thought I might lose my eyesight along with everything else. Finally, a kind nurse came into my room and downed me with a good dose of Lorazepam, then she touched me on my cheek and said, 'It's not so bad, at least you're not in a coma.'

In the morning, feeling rather peckish, I was encouraged by the pleasant breakfast smells wafting in from the corridor. I was delighted to see, for the first time, an array of hot Italian pastries and cheeses and some freshly squeezed orange juice.

The nurses have to feed me. This particular one didn't speak English and was apparently unaware of my requirements. The food sat there on my table temptingly for an hour before the nurse returned, shrugged, picked up the tray and asked, 'You did not like?' before leaving with my breakfast.

Later, one of the physios came to see me. A serious man with dark eyes who promised that I would raise a pen again with my right hand. I find this difficult to believe; at present my fingers resemble sausages sewn to the stump of my wrist.

Tomorrow I will be leaving here. This is my last day in this little room, my temporary prison. I will be moved to a much larger six-floor facility where they say I will receive high-quality physiotherapy. It feels as if my body is turning into marshmallow, that I am deliquescing. I will also be able to meet others whose bodies are busted in different ways.

A strange thing happened to me: I went to Rome with Isabella for a few days at Christmas and now I will never go home again. I have no home now, no centre. I am a stranger to myself. I don't know who I am any more. Someone new is emerging.

The thing I miss most from my former life is reading. Being in my study, wandering around, picking up a book from here or there; a work of fiction, an autobiography, history, some psycho-analysis. I like reading in this kind of random way, and find it to be a form of self-communing.

Reading and writing go hand in hand for me. I was encouraged to write by my father when I was a young man; we discussed structure, char-acters, meaning and ideas, notions that continue to fascinate me. What does and does not make a piece of writing work? I'm watching a lot of television now and find most of it unoriginal and unadventurous. The era of neoliberalism in creative writing has somehow convinced people that you can purchase the ability to write. To a certain extent you can, but you can only buy the obvious things, like formula. With real writ-ing, there is contact between the deepest part of one person and that of another. You should take it for granted that the reader has a sympathetic ear; that they will receive your words kindly and with interest, just as you might listen to them.

It is time for my second enema now. I am looking forward to it.

13/01/2023

SANTA LUCIA HOSPITAL, ROME

I wake at four in the morning knowing I will be moving today. I wonder what the place will be like.

At five, my favourite doctor arrives. He is shy and intelligent, and we begin our daily chat. We discuss my legs, Giorgia Meloni, the upbringing of teenagers and the pleasure of when your children become your friends.

He tells me that Russian novels were originally translated into French before being turned into English. He asks me to recommend a good translation of Proust's *Remembrance of Things Past*.

I show him a photograph of my psychoanalyst and suggest some books by him. The doctor breaks a sugary biscuit into murky tea and feeds me while he tells me the story of being taken to Calabria to perform surgery on a Mafia don. The experience surprised him because despite the great wealth of the Mafioso, they appeared to have quite squalid lives. You would have thought, he said, they would have better taste in carpets. We continue to talk for an hour about this and that. It is wonderful to have found such a companion. I ask him what worries him most. He says the future of Italy.

I have to say that becoming paralysed is a great way to meet new people.

My family and the doctors have discussed my next move. We have agreed that I should delay my return to London as there are ambulance strikes, I am also too fragile for such a move, and don't have travel insurance. Instead, I will transfer to the Santa Lucia Hospital on the outskirts of Rome, an advanced facility that specializes in rehab for spinal cord injuries, among other things. It is also helpful for Isabella to remain here in her native Rome since she will have the support of her friends and family. Her life has been upended by this accident; she spends every minute of visiting hours at my side, before going to her mother's each evening for supper. With a friend she runs a small PR agency for writers and festivals, which she has more or less abandoned to take care of me.

Isabella and I leave my room and are taken by ambulance to the new hospital. I am lying on a stretcher, but through the windows I catch a glimpse of the blazing blue sky.

The Santa Lucia is a huge, modern 1980s building, high-tech, with a large green lawn in front of it. The place could be the setting for a Ballardesque sci-fi movie.

My new room is wide, comfortable and non-descript. Across the room is another bed with a man asleep in it. Isabella feeds me some lunch and I ingest a rather large piece of fish. Seconds later, I am choking. Isabella cries for help and four nurses run in and after some clapping on my back the fish is out of me. The doctor tells me I could have died at any moment. I'll take it easy with the fish in future.

A man comes in with a measuring tape and says he's checking my size for the wheelchair.

I feel depressed. I am in despair, I don't want to be here, I want to go home, I'd rather die now.

I've had enough of this shit. I feel I lack the strength to take this on. I really don't want to live like this. It's shit and I'm tired of asking Isabella to do so much for me. Then, a wheelchair-bound woman in her late thirties, with long dyed bright-blue hair, rolls herself into the room and we introduce ourselves. I'll call her Miss S.

I ask if we can be friends. I plead with her to not let me go. She tells me she won't. She says, 'After my accident, when I first came here, I could only use one eye.'

14/01/2023

Sleepless night. Not a moment's rest. Racing mind. I wake up with an elevated temperature and fear of an infection. Blood in the urine.

A new catheter and a massive pain in the genitals. An anaesthetic in the penis. A visit to the laryngologist after the incident with the fish and the Heimlich manoeuvre. Tubes up the nose and down the throat and a sore arse.

A pop-in from my new friend, a fellow patient of my age, a man I call the Maestro, an actor and director who rolls into my room wearing a capacious hoodie and brings me a cappuccino, feeding it to me through a straw. His experiences have been much worse than mine, almost unendurable: a cancer diagnosis, numerous operations, as well as a spinal injury.

Physios come and pull and push, prod and twist me. My body feels battered and broken.

16/01/2023

Someone must have listened to my complaints because the doctors upped my sleeping dosage. I slept until 4 a.m. My new room-mate talked throughout the night in his sleep, of course in Italian. I can't say he bothered me. You can get used to anything.

I have watched all of *Breaking Bad* twice and some episodes several times. Anthony Hopkins said that he thought Bryan Cranston's performance as Walter White was the greatest he had ever seen, and Hopkins would know.

The writing and intelligence of the show is of the highest quality in any genre, if you ask me. Now that I have free evenings, I am watching the *Breaking Bad* spin-off, *Better Call Saul*.

Bob Odenkirk's depiction of the confused genius Jimmy McGill is masterful. Jonathan Banks's portrayal of Mike Ehrmantraut, the melancholic private investigator and fixer, is played with profound poise. These shows are worth watching over and over.

I guess the whole point of acting is that you don't notice it. But when you do, as in the case of Jonathan Banks, you enjoy it as you would the work of any great artist. Hats off to the man.

At mid-morning three nurses came to the room pushing a human-carrying machine, a hoist, which resembles a small crane. They dress me; it's the first time I've worn clothes since my accident. I am even wearing shoes.

The nurses attach me to the machine, which lifts me from my bed. For a few moments I hang in the air like a fly, my limbs dangling down beneath me. Then the hoist drops me nicely into a wheelchair.

My friend the Maestro spins in with my cappuccino. We then have a heated conversation with the doctor about how Americans drink cappuccinos at inappropriate times of the day.

The doctor said he had even heard of an American who had once requested a cappuccino in the evening. The Maestro could not believe that such a thing had happened. It would be like putting jam on pasta, he said.

Then I am swept through the myriad wide

corridors and halls of this vast contemporary hospital to the gym. It is huge, well lit and equipped with numerous technical-looking machines. I should add here that this is the first time I have ever been in a gym.

They push me towards the window and I look out at the sky, the trees and hospital garden. I am not joking when I say that a surge of passion passes through me like an electrical current.

This is when I decide I want to become an Italian citizen, with an Italian passport. I will apply for one tomorrow. How could anyone not want to live in Italy? I will discuss it later with Isabella, who is always a wise guide to reality, and will inform me if I am pushing the limits of my sanity.

I work in the gym with the physio for an hour or so and I feel different parts of my body starting to respond. This has been the best day so far. Later, when I return to my room feeling high and feverish, a doctor asks me if I would be interested in participating in an international study they are conducting on those with spinal injuries. Having always wanted to be a subject in a medical experiment, I am enthusiastic.

I will get two extra hours of physio every day. The idea is to see how much difference this makes to my development.

17/01/2023

One of the things about lying in a hospital bed for hours on end is that you start to remember in a way you didn't before, often in elaborate detail. Past events return seemingly at random. If you have no future, the past comes back to you.

I was happily watching *Better Call Saul* when the iPad stopped working. The screen went black and a legend appeared, asking: 'Are you still there?' Now, that is an interesting question.

I attempted to grab a damp straw between my teeth and answer in the affirmative. The straw was no good. I then tried pressing my somewhat bulbous Indian nose against the screen but succeeded only in pushing the iPad further away.

The legend remained. Was I still there? Was I anywhere?

My room-mate has been sleeping a lot, often noiselessly, which is a mercy. But when he does snore, in our shared darkened room, his grunts sound like a sea lion.

I have eaten in fine restaurants. I have dined with scientists, artists and Brian Eno. But spending every night six feet from this injured man, his wails and incessant night-time phone calls, is new to me. I have no beef with him, nor he with me. Our lives have become intertwined.

When my dear late friend the director Roger Michell and I wrote together – we worked on six films – we devised a system called the Queenie Leavis Merit of Marking when evaluating scenes. It involved three designations of distinction; the first was Naughty, the second was Double Naughty, and the third Triple Naughty.

Each scene would receive its mark. In our film *Venus* there was a scene between Vanessa Redgrave and Peter O'Toole which we considered Triple Naughty. O'Toole's character apologizes for his bad behaviour to his wife before saying goodbye, as he believed he was dying. We deemed this scene Triple Naughty because something beautiful happened between the actors; they elevated the dialogue and created something exquisite out of it.

I considered O'Toole a bit of a cunt despite his fine acting. Everyone around him did their best not to provoke or annoy him. He said to me, 'The only Paki I ever liked was Omar Sharif.' I said, 'It's a bit of a stretch to consider Omar Sharif a Paki but at least one of you was probably a gentleman.' On set O'Toole was known as Florence of Arabia.

I wonder if there is a sexual fantasy I can return to. Ah yes; in 2004 I gave a reading in Amsterdam. In a bar at the end of the night, a Dutch woman in her mid-twenties asked me to sleep with her, and she rode me to my hotel on the back of her huge Dutch bicycle.

A year later, I went back to Amsterdam and rang her up. I invited her to pass by. She could do some shopping on the way if she had the time, bringing a couple of joints, magic mushrooms, lingerie and some chocolate for when we got the munchies. 'Anything else?' she asked. I told her to bring a friend. 'Sure. See you soon.'

If this was a film, the camera would be

close on Isabella's face as she writes this down for me.

After a few hours there was a knock on my hotel door. In my boxers and loose-fitting shirt, I opened up and there she was, let's call her Iris, with all the contraband, and the friend.

I'll finish this story later.

18/01/2023

Yesterday, before lunch, I was elevated from my bed and slid into my wheelchair. My two new best friends, Miss S and the Maestro, gathered at the door of my room for a trip out.

They had arranged for someone equipped with the necessary two legs to push me to the bar of the clinic where the three of us would have a view of the hospital garden and some sheep on the hill in the distance.

At the café we had cappuccino and cake. As patients tend to, we discussed the various drugs we ingest every day; whether they are useful or not and how to get more of them according to our needs.

The Maestro had taken peyote in Mexico, according to the ceremony. He tripped out in Nepal. He was a racing driver in Los Angeles. I like his stories.

I am keen that Isabella knows that I am capable of making new friends. Indeed, when I think about it, I wonder how long it has been since I made a new friend that I liked and who liked me. Over the last five years I have really only seen old friends and my family. I guess it didn't occur to me that I could be interested in someone new.

I woke up this morning thinking about my old life and how dull it was. I wonder whether I enjoyed the repetition of it or whether I had just become lazy. Boredom has a lot going for it. Many writers, from Kafka to Beckett, have taken it as their subject. I was wondering about Dickens as a writer of boring people. But his boring characters are not boring at all; they are idiots, cretins or intriguing grotesques. For me, the writer who specializes in boredom, and in boring people, is Chekhov, who even had the balls to write a story with the title 'A Boring Story'.

There are bores in all his plays, and he doesn't spare us the details. This person, he says to us, has almost crushed me to death with the weight of their interminable words, and now onstage, even as you pay to watch it, I am going to do the same to you.

What writing teacher, in giving their finest

advice, would ever recommend to a young writer that they deliberately create some of the most tedious people on earth?

I discussed this question with my two new best friends who both agree that boring people can be extremely popular, particularly as bosses.

My mother was the most boring person I ever met. Because I was a child, I had no choice but to spend many seconds, minutes, hours and years with her. She had not the slightest interest in charming or entertaining anyone, least of all me.

She was not mean, cruel or uncompassionate. In fact, she could be kind and charitable, and she worked once a week in the Oxfam shop on Bromley High Street for years. But what she wanted was to reduce the atmosphere around her to an extreme inertia where nothing was alive or could flourish. She spoke in clichés. In fact she spoke in nothing but clichés; it was as if she were reading from a ticker-tape of platitudes.

Harold Pinter used many common clichés to powerful and dramatic effect, but for my poor mother this was communication itself. She must have felt dead. She wanted to be dead, and she conveyed to us quite clearly that that is how she felt.

I guess this is commonly known as depression. In her more lively moments she would describe herself as placid.

My father was a well-read, witty and cultured man. He earned a living and did most of the housework. Despite being a Muslim father, he was a whizz with the Hoover. He did the dusting.

He says several times in his diaries, which I was rereading recently, that he loved my mother but found her frustrating and rigid. But he never thought either of leaving her or finding someone of better character.

I wonder whether other parents and their marriages are equally baffling to their children. As a child, my father was my hero, and still is. The other day, before my accident, I began to think I was turning into my mother.

She had one lifelong friend and she succeeded in turning that friendship into a tedious dispute. Liking other people was one thing she couldn't bear.

If you started liking people, if there was excitement, anything could happen. And where might you go next? She was frightened, terrified her whole life.

In my fiction I have attempted to characterize her several times, but I always made her too interesting or tried to inject her with some vigour. Getting her right would have required more care from me as a writer. More Chekhovian exactness.

I have received a massive blow across the head and entered a new reality. Miss S said this morning that hospital is often painful and boring, but it is usually interesting.

Thirty years ago, my analyst told me to say almost everything that came into my mind. That was the analytic rule, but it could equally apply to everyday life. He would say that you could never know how the other would respond, that they could surprise you too. My mother never wanted to be surprised. Now I want nothing but surprises.

19/01/2023

Yesterday there was a catastrophe. We wrote a dispatch and then lost it in the internet ether. I am sure all of you have had this experience. It is tiring doing this work and there were tears and recriminations when I accused Isabella of going the full Bette Davis. She said I behaved as if I, Marcel Proust, had written *Remembrance of Things Past* on a toilet roll on which a rent boy had wiped his arse.

This morning Miss S and the Maestro came to my room for a coffee trip to the bar, but the nurse said he was busy and could not push me there.

So Miss S got behind me, and behind her was the Maestro, and the two of them, in this wagon-train of wheelchairs, pushed me all the way to the bar where we had an Italian orange-flavoured drink called Crodino and white pizza.

Having promised myself as a young man never to drink anything orange, I did in fact enjoy the Crodino, which tastes a little like

Lucozade. As you can see, I have become a man of flexible principles.

The good news is I have a new mattress. Apparently, there is some envy on the other wards because these good new mattresses are difficult to acquire. People think I am behaving like a VIP because I keep a dispatch about life in here and going to the bar.

I can tell you that the new mattress is like lying between the breasts of Jayne Mansfield and there is no way I would forfeit it. If I am not on the mattress I have a tremendous pain in the arse, wherever else I sit. I can tell you that a pain in the arse is a pain in the arse.

This morning a nurse was washing me while singing a song by Abba called 'Fernando'. As he sang, he got my shit on his fingers and said to me, 'I thought that was going to happen – I have a good nose,' and kept on singing.

When I went to the gym this afternoon and saw all the patients with their broken or mal-formed bodies being manipulated and caressed by the physiotherapists, something in me changed.

I thought, if you only watch the news and TV shows, you would have the impression that the world is a harsh place, inhabited by money-grubbing and narcissistic criminals. When you see the mutual work done in the gym, it is a place of beauty, collaboration and respect.

Many of the patients I have spoken to are aware that those in the outside world are appalled by, if not afraid of, those with disabilities. It is as if having a disability were contagious, which it is.

Most of us at some time in our lives will suffer from a catastrophic health crisis that will make us feel isolated and afraid. We want to believe we live in a world of healthy and well-functioning people, having convinced ourselves that there is a standard of the effective human being. This is a deception, a misleading ideology. It means we cannot always see the disabled, just as in other circumstances we fail to see those of colour, or queers. We should give up this standardized view of the world for a more complex idea, which will include more people.

*

The Hungarian psychoanalyst Sándor Ferenczi wrote a paper about remarkable children who have been traumatized. The trauma, according to him, produces a rapid growth spurt because the child has to develop fast in order to comprehend and organize themself around the new horror.

I am aware of this in my own life; as a teenager I was so traumatized by racism and the unpleasantness of school that I began to read and write at a remarkable rate. You could say that trauma saved me and made me into a writer. Something similar is happening here: I am finding a way to cope with the shock of my recent accident by writing through dictation.

21/01/2023

After the incident involving the fish, I am now more intimate with the Heimlich manoeuvre than I am with cunnilingus. It doesn't follow that just because you are severely injured, you don't think about sex. Indeed you might think about it more.

Eventually, I could be capable of a little light cunnilingus, and I hope I will be. But right now I am a desperate man attempting to open a bag of cashews using only my teeth and a brick wall for purchase.

I can't help but envy able-bodied sexual beings, and envy is an animating force. I remember as a child, in my local park in Bromley, being jealous of other kids who were better at football, and who earned trials at Crystal Palace and Millwall.

When I was around the age of fourteen, my best friend's mother gave her son, with some despair, an acoustic guitar, telling him to 'Get on with it.' I guess she thought, if the kid is good for nothing else, he might at least find his place in one of these horrible bands, where the talentless become rich and famous.

I learned to play the guitar around the same time. I practised a lot at home and read guitar books. When my friend and I decided to form a group called the Orange Socks, I soon saw that he was already a far better guitarist than I would ever be.

So what to do, then? Give up or persist? Wisely, I gave up. I envied him a bit but my envy got me nowhere.

As I moved beyond my teenage years, I had an outbreak of many other envies. I envied those who could make good jokes. I envied other boys who could speak to women without defecating. And I envied those who were good at maths and science, which I found tedious and lacking in actual flesh-and-blood life.

But to my own surprise, I persisted in looking for something I might be better at than others. I did eventually find something I was more than half-good at, which is writing. And I can still do it, fluently, up to a certain level. It is a talent you must practise daily, like a dancer or sportsperson, but at base it is a gift, and as such it is inexplicable. No one can say why someone is a brilliant artist, while someone else, equally intelligent, has no imagination.

You would think at my age that I would be free of the disease of envy. But this morning, with my two new friends at the hospital bar, as they attempted to teach me backgammon, I found myself acknowledging a newfound sense of envy.

I envy those who can scratch their own heads. I envy those who can tie their own shoe-laces. I envy those who can pick up a cup of coffee. When I saw a man waving to his own wife, I couldn't believe that he didn't see what a profoundly complicated act this was. I envy anyone who can use their own hands.

Yesterday, in the gym, my physiotherapist placed my right claw-like hand on to my cheek. It was dreadful, lifeless, as if a dead man's hand had fallen into my face. The hand felt cold and inanimate. But Miss S claims I should forgo the self-pity. If I persist with my exercises I will be waving at London taxis and giving my enemies the finger in no time. At the moment, my right hand is livelier than my left, which feels numb and full of pins and needles – a connection interrupted.

What I would like – what I wish for, what I dream of – is the ability to pick up a fountain pen and make a mark on the page; to write my own name in purple ink. This is my ambition.

22/01/2023

Being a tetraplegic isn't all bad. As I write this, I am having a pedicure while eating caviar with a plastic spoon, Isabella is tickling me under the chin. I have just proposed to her. 'Barkis is willin'.'

While she pretends to contemplate the question — to my surprise, and that of most of my friends, who consider me to be less than a good catch, in fact a bad catch, and had advised me against proposing while I am in this condition — she eventually says yes and laughs.

Isabella and I first met in Rome in the mid-1990s when my novel *Intimacy* was published by Bompiani, my long-term Italian publisher. As my publicist, she and I attended many festivals together as well as parties given by the British Council in Rome. It was a bucolic and lovely time. I had money, I was successful, and my books did well. Over lunches and drinks I enjoyed her company more and more. Her father, an academic, translator, theatre critic and keen Roma supporter, was charming and became a good friend. I learned about her family: her paternal grandmother, Suso Cecchi d'Amico, was a prolific screenwriter, working with De Sica on *Bicycle Thieves*, and Visconti on *Rocco and His Brothers* and *The Leopard*, among other things. In 2012 we were in Milan, chatting in my hotel room, when I asked her if she wanted to be my girlfriend. We became a couple, and three years later she moved to London, where we began to live together.

Having grown up in the 1960s, I never thought of marriage as much of an aspiration. But now I've changed my mind. If I get out of this mess, I'd like to mark our love for one another.

Meanwhile, I'm having my first ever pedicure. The man doing it at the end of my bed wears a sort of miner's harness on his forehead with a bright little torch attached.

From where I am lying, with his whirring machine and his glasses covered in foot-dust, he resembles someone cleaning the inside of a nuclear dump.

In the gym today a man tried to sell me a horse. He showed me a picture of the horse. I can confirm the horse is very pretty. I had to explain to him my garden in London is not big enough for a horse. Like you, I was wondering whether this patient became paralysed after being kicked in the back by said horse. But there is an etiquette when it comes to other patients' injuries. You have to know them reasonably well before asking about their accidents.

My physiotherapist hoists me from my chair and lays me on a plinth. He begins to work on my arms and legs, stretching and assessing me, to find out what my range of movements is. As he pulls at me, he says that many of the younger patients here have had motorcycle accidents. The public transport system in Rome is inefficient and the best way for young people to get about is to use motorcycles, which are dangerous because the roads, like a lot of the public realm, are in bad condition and full of potholes.

I know I am being cared for in this hospital but I feel as if I am living in an authoritarian regime. The people who work here are not tyrannical. What I mean is that my body is constantly being invaded: someone comes into my room and inserts a needle into my arm, while another nurse sticks one in my stomach, and finally a tube is shoved into my arse. I have also had two injections of cortisone in my backside, which may have contributed to my elevated mood.

Then I am dragged in my bed to a room at the far side of the hospital, where a man hits me over the head twenty times with a large magnetic ping-pong bat, for my own good. I feel like Jack Nicholson at the end of *One Flew Over the Cuckoo's Nest*, writhing in despair and helplessness.

I've been told that swimming – hydrotherapy – could be beneficial for me. I am in the gym, lying on a plinth in my swimming trunks, being stretched by my physio Fabio, when a nurse approaches. She draws the plastic curtain around me for privacy, puts on rubber gloves, and sticks her finger up my arse to ascertain, as she puts it, whether I am clean enough to go in the pool. After she examines her finger,

I get the all-clear, and she proceeds to insert a butt plug into my rectum to ensure I don't leak. This is the protocol every time I do hydrotherapy. On the following two occasions, I am not considered clean enough, and I am infuriated. After a time, tired of all this up-the-arseness, I tell them I no longer wish to do hydrotherapy, and that is that.

I am feeling highly sartorial today. I am wearing my new white Snoopy socks, my black Uniqlo sports pants; on top, I have a long-sleeve striped 'Picasso' T-shirt, and over that, an off-white Gap hoodie.

On my head, I have an ochre woollen hat. When I catch a glimpse of myself in the mirror, I am as enthusiastic and disappointed as any teenager.

I have been thinking a lot about my look, which is strange, since from the shoulders up, unshaven and with straggly hair, I resemble a man who has just run out of a burning building – his own house.

In the evenings, at home in the mid-1960s,

I would watch my father prepare his work clothes for the following morning. I would help him decide which shirt, tie or suit he would wear. These were 'groovy' times and my father was proud of his look; it took him ages to get ready.

Aware of the psychedelic era in which we were living, and with money from my daily paper round, I would buy the cheap vibrant clothes which best expressed my identifications. We all had a look then, there were many tribes in the South London suburbs: mods, rockers, hippies, Teds, and so on. Every stitch you wore was a signifier that marked you out. I wore my grandfather's tie-dyed vests, my father's sequinned Indian waistcoats and his loafers, and velvet flares I had picked up somewhere on Bromley High Street. After this, I was never not concerned with my look; wherever I was, whatever I was doing, I wanted to be someone.

So this morning, as I lay on my back in the gym, I was planning my next ensemble, which Isabella can acquire for me on the streets of Rome.

As I prepare for life as a married man, I am wondering what colour to paint my nails. The colours that I have suggested – which include the colours of my team, Manchester United – have been considered by Isabella with some restrained hilarity.

Here in the hospital, I am seen by many women – nurses, doctors, patients and visitors. But because most of them are wearing masks, I can only study their eyes, hair and eyebrows. I have to confess, I have acquired a knowledge of the Italian eyebrow which is extensive and detailed. Each eyebrow is, of course, a story and an artwork in itself. One of the nurses here, Roberta – who used to work in movies, in hair and make-up – told me that the eyebrow is the most important feature of the face.

She added: the public might not notice it, but the eyebrow of the villain in any movie has to be paid special attention to, as it must emphasize a 'wrong'un'.

I should stress here that the Italian male also attends to his eyebrows with calculated care, not something I have noticed in the British male. We are more primitive, except in British soap operas, where the male eyebrow seems to be given particular scrutiny.

Italian women take good care of themselves. Everything about them is neat and planned, and the women who are not in work uniform – the visitors – exude stylish confidence with their vivid, clashing colours.

When it comes to myself – who I am, and who I might become – I want to return to the late 1960s and early 1970s, when I was growing up. I guess most people, of whatever age, wear the clothes of their youth. I will be doing this, with the volume turned up, and with super-painted toenails. But first I need to get home.

30/01/2023

As a young man, I loved to look at photographs of writers I admired: Henry Miller, Raymond Chandler, Jean Rhys, Dashiell Hammett, Anaïs Nin and Simone de Beauvoir. But my hero in literary terms, and sartorially, was Graham Greene.

To be honest, there is no reason for a writer to look good. When we are working, no one needs to look at us, tapping away in our pyjamas in our little rooms. And when we are not working, it is better that we fade into the background, as we are observers and not movie stars.

Speaking of movies and movie stars.

Billy Wilder. Bogart. City of Night. The Doors. Sunset Strip. My first trip to Los Angeles after having been, to my surprise – and to that of director Stephen Frears – nominated for an Oscar, in 1985, for my first film, *My Beautiful Laundrette*.

My then girlfriend, Sally, and I had been living a quiet life in a tiny, one-bedroom housing association flat in Barons Court, West Kensington. She, a left-wing, feminist social worker, and me, more of an opportunist social climber, working backstage at various theatres, including Riverside Studios and the Royal Court. Now we are checking in to the Chateau Marmont in Hollywood, also known as 'Hotel California' after the Eagles song. A period of impossible fulfilment and vertigo.

I've already written *Sammy and Rosie Get Laid*, the next film I will do with Stephen Frears. Here, in LA, I have an agent and I go to meetings. I am offered work. I meet other British writers working in Hollywood as rewrite specialists. Some are employed just to revise the endings of movies. Others are better at the beginnings. I wonder who writes the middle.

Despite the weather, these British writers seem pallid, confused and agitated. They are earning good money, and hustling for bigger gigs, but I wonder if they know who they are, and what they are really doing. In truth, they are hired hands who are given a brief and must fulfil it.

I am approached by Costa-Gavras, a distinguished Greek movie director whose films I admire. He takes me for lunch at the Four Seasons, and then for a walk along Venice Beach, where we watch the muscle Marys working out.

I begin to realize he is interviewing me as a possible writer for his new movie set in apartheid South Africa. But I do not want to be interviewed. I don't necessarily want to write his new movie – though, from another point of view, it would be a privilege. He works with the best actors.

But I don't know what I should be doing next and I am annoyed at myself. I become frustrated with him, I am not a mercenary, I think I want to be a novelist. I want to write what will become *The Buddha of Suburbia*, but I am not sure how to start.

Years later, my first son, Sachin, and I write a film together, soon after he finishes university. It is partly based on his experience working as a driver for a rock star. It almost got made and, to my pleasure, he decided that he wanted to become a screenwriter. Off this, he was offered a job on a well-known British soap opera.

Earning good money and learning a lot, it was a great gig for a young writer, developing him as a professional, as someone who could work under pressure and meet deadlines. I began to watch the soap opera every night, and even when he left the show, I continued to watch it.

Now, being in Italy, I miss it. I wonder how the characters are doing. The soap opera is obviously the most ludicrous and artificial of all literary forms. One day there is an earthquake, the next a fire, a murder, a bombing, and so on.

But there is something about the form that works, which is addictive. Despite its absurdities, or because of them, there is something about the characters' anguish that is recognizable.

The reason I bring this up is that after I left Los Angeles – when I returned to London without an Oscar but with several job proposals, one of which was a good gig on *Doctor Who* – I turned all this work down.

What sort of writer did I want to be, and how would I find out? Did I want to be a screenwriter at all? After all, the screenwriter is mostly subordinate to the director, the producer, and even to the actors.

I guess I followed my instinct. I would write as myself, in my own voice. Just because Franz Kafka was a talented writer, it wouldn't follow that he could write a good Donald Duck movie, or Samuel Beckett work for Billy Wilder.

I think I realized in Los Angeles that I was a British writer and that race and the legacy of colonialism would be my subject. And so, after working on a movie, *London Kills Me*, about a rapidly gentrifying Notting Hill – an area that would soon become a millionaires' playground – I switched tracks and decided I should write a novel, using my own life as a template.

After all, Graham Greene, who looked suave whether he was in Africa, Cuba or Clapham, wrote at least two very fine movies, many novels, essays and short stories, to a high standard. I wanted to explore other forms. At this time, the novel suited me because there were no collaborators.

I loved the singular voice. Think of *David Copperfield*, *The Catcher in the Rye*, *Portnoy's Complaint* and *The Bell Jar*.

In each of these, the point of view drives the story forward; you want to spend time with the characters, you love their company, and will follow them where they want to take you, even if you find them deplorable. Any novel could be as short, as long or as eccentric as you like. I would abandon screenwriting and have a go at this. I began as a novelist and, after a long detour, I wanted to find my way back.

I had been travelling a lot, with *My Beautiful Laundrette*, introducing the film all over the world and giving interviews. Wherever I was, I started to buy books, published in the 1960s and up to the mid-1970s.

These were books about encounter groups: Taoism, Zen, the Esalen Institute in California, Fritz Perls, Gestalt therapy, and other forms of semi-hippy self-transformation.

Zen in the Art of Archery had a particular

influence on me. All this came out of my father's interest in Buddhism and would later function as background to the character of the father in *The Buddha of Suburbia*. As I was preparing to write this novel, I also wanted to free myself from my adolescent fears and inhibitions.

I considered myself to be a nervous, if not uptight, and repressed person. I could speak onstage, but found it difficult to be intimate with others. In the suburbs, where I was brought up, silence, if not shyness, was a virtue.

I wanted to use a freer voice, not unlike that of Henry Miller, writing the words that were somehow getting stuck or jammed up in my head. I wondered whether the restrained part of me might contain some of my most interesting ideas.

I originally started to write *The Buddha of Suburbia* in the third person – *he did this, he did that*. But it didn't work and I laboured on it for a while. When I turned it into a first-person narrative, the book took off, becoming more lively and true.

I took ideas from real people, bits and pieces

here and there, but most characters in a novel are lifted from a number of sources, and in the end it all becomes fictionalized. There are events that did happen to real people I knew: Karim's visit to Helen's house, her father setting the dog on him, clambering over the fence to escape with the hound's semen on his jeans – that did actually occur how I wrote it, and it certainly wasn't funny at the time. I always advise my students to write as freely as they can, taking whatever they want from real life. Later, they can change the circumstances of the characters so they won't be recognizable; it is easy to do. When you are writing a book, the main purpose is to delight the reader: that should be the focus of the work.

The Buddha is a kind of picaresque: not a story based around plot, but one which leaps from incident to incident, as the character develops and matures.

I was aware at the time that it was the first novel about a person like me. There had been plenty of *growing-up* novels written since the war, but oddly enough, no one in Britain was writing about Asian immigrants. In the previous decades, the country had transformed because of people like my father and other immigrants from the Caribbean, Bangladesh and India. They had landed, settled and had children; some of whom had grown up mixed-raced, as I am. But their stories were yet to be told. There was a new demographic here, accompanied by massive social change; whole cities were altering in their racial and religious make-up. Political figures like Enoch Powell had commented on the situation, but there was little fiction you could read to find out about the inner lives of immigrants and their families, their children, their hopes and ambitions, and what it was like to move from a former colony to the mother country. So I began to understand that these would be dramatic, exciting and moving stories about a social revolution. I wrote the book as quickly as I could, for fear there was somebody around the corner writing another one and would get there first. I had already read Salman Rushdie's remarkable *Midnight's Children*, and that book had created a literary stir and won the Booker

Prize. He was a good friend to me, an encour-
ager, and a fine example to follow. But he wasn't
at that time writing about Britain. So, I picked
up my favourite fountain pen, the Mont Blanc,
and began . . .

31/01/2023

It's not unpleasant here. The doctors, nurses and all the workers are kind. Almost all of them look you in the eye and at least smile. They know that they have to relate to each patient. They aren't afraid of touching the most abhorrent, aged or broken body. But what still makes me despair is the idea that I can't walk up the front path of my house, open the door, and step back into my old life – lie down on my sofa, with a glass of wine and the Premier League. It seems unbelievably cruel that I cannot do such a simple thing.

I had my accident on Boxing Day. What's that – about a month and a half ago? This is a fact that is unbearable, a stone so hard and round that I can't swallow it or spit it out. It's as if I have been plucked off the street by four anonymous policemen and been taken to a strange school: an irrational, persecutory alternative universe. I have to find a way to survive, like we all did when we were children. I need to make friends; I've got to figure out how the system functions.

I want to be a good patient and to be recognized as a polite and decent man. I want to ask everyone their name, their story and why they chose this job. At other times, I'm too tired for this rigmarole.

I recently had a discussion on the phone with my schoolfriend David of Bromley. I put to him that old cliché, 'Why me?' He replied, 'Why not you? Whyever would you think it would not be you?'

His brother was killed in a motorcycle accident; David himself was almost killed in a motorcycle crash, he was eighteen and inches from death.

Many of us expect one day to be acknowledged for our exceptional qualities, but Kafka points out that we may be noticed only for our ordinariness, for the fact that we are not much more than nothing in the universe, though we may be important to one another, if we are lucky. Death staring you in the face renders you less inhibited than you might have been before.

It is not so difficult to become intimate with strangers. I knew Neil Kinnock, former leader of the Labour Party, in the late 1980s. He was a charming and intelligent man, and taught me how to ask anyone where they came from, where they live and who their parents were – how to get a measure of anyone in ten minutes. Several direct questions can create a bridge between people, the illusion of knowing. It is easy to do. Sometimes too easy, if you think of it as a form of seduction. People are keener than you might think to tell you about themselves. They want to be known and recognized. This is the basis of psychoanalysis: questions which provoke a chain of free associations.

My dad used to say if you wanted to write an article for a newspaper you had to use the *who what when where why* principle. These fundamental questions are also the basis of fiction. You must interrogate your characters – they must live in a recognizable world.

04/02/2023

Last night was a bad one. A bit of a stand-off at two in the morning with a nurse. I wanted more sleeping pills and he insisted I had had enough already.

Of course I have my own stash at Isabella's apartment – antihistamines, temazepam, beta-blockers, weed – but I do not have access to it. And if I started mixing this stuff, I could go up like kerosene.

The nurse suggested I should lie still with my eyes closed. It sounded like good advice. I tried it for two or three hours, but found my mind was going faster and faster. Since my accident, I seem to be working harder, writing more than I have for years, with more determination and ferocity.

My mind frequently returns to my childhood. I was born in the mid-1950s and grew up in a small but comfortable house with a large garden where I would play cricket with my father, who came from a notable Bombay cricketing family. I was named after the great Pakistani opening batsman Hanif Mohammad, whose powers of concentration were apparently incredible: he could bat for three days straight, and once scored 499 runs in a first-class match.

Most of the men in our neighbourhood had jobs rather than careers or professions. But some of them were teachers, civil servants or solicitors. The man who lived directly across the road from us, in our cul-de-sac, worked as a printer in Fleet Street. Next to him there was a motor mechanic, known as Motorbike Bill. Further down the street was another man who sold bird food. There were many commuters, like my dad, in our neighbourhood. Around six thirty in the morning, getting up for my paper round, I would hear my father downstairs washing himself. He would shave twice and put on his suit. He would then sit down at his typewriter and work on a novel about his privileged upbringing in Bombay. He had eleven siblings. His father was a colonel and doctor in the British army. As a family, we hated colonialism but not the British themselves, of whom many were our friends.

Dad would finish writing, pack his briefcase and walk to the bus stop. From there he would take the bus to Bromley South station, before changing to the fast train to Victoria. From Victoria he would walk to the Pakistan High Commission in Lowndes Square, Knights-bridge. Since this was the 1960s and there were a lot of Pakistanis coming to the UK, some of them working for a short time at the embassy, I began to hear fascinating stories of Britain's multiracial transformation. Stories of racism and hardship, but also stories of arranged mar-riages, Indian restaurants, corner shops, factory workers, families beginning to buy properties, and the new communities emerging around what was then known as London Airport, now Heathrow.

At weekends, we would visit friends in the slums of Herne Hill and Brixton. I heard anec-dotes that I knew I would like to use in fiction: stories of real life, social change and conflict, yet to be told. I knew that when I developed my craft as a writer, and some sensibility as a human being, this would be my material. It was original. It felt like an opportunity.

One of the most important parts of any writer's capability is the discovery of their subject matter. It could be Clapham for Graham Greene or Paris for Jean Rhys or Henry Miller. I have known young writers of great ability who hadn't yet discovered the theme that would bring their talent to life.

My father's job was boring and exhausting, and in the end it kind of killed him. But he had no choice in the matter; he needed to support my mother, my sister and me. He wanted me to be a professional cricketer, to be the first Pakistani to play for England. We would train for hours in the garden. He was an excellent teacher, but although I loved to watch cricket I hated to play. I was frightened by the ball and scared of my father recognizing my cowardice. He admired fearless small batsmen like Rohan Kanhai and Javed Miandad, men who batted against the world's fastest bowlers without protection.

The hook was my father's favourite shot and he made me practise it for hours. To this day I have images of my head exploding under the impact of a hundred-mile-an-hour hurtling cricket ball. I hate cricket now and can barely stand to watch it.

05/02/2023

Shit and piss.

Miss S and the Maestro come to visit me, and I am keen to see them, but the conversation is almost entirely about shit and shitting.

They are in the process of trying to shit independently, which means transferring from their wheelchairs to the toilet and out of their nappies. This is a big step in the life of some of the patients here.

But both of them have had disastrous toilet accidents. They shat on the floor, which isn't so unusual at this stage. But the Maestro is stressed and humiliated, and now begins to weep.

Miss S tells him not to be silly; it's part of the development; there can be no progress without failure. But the Maestro continues to take this badly. He goes to bed with an infection. We don't see him for several days, and we worry. Then Miss S gets an infection, which again isn't so unusual in hospital.

As for my arse, you will be fascinated to hear

that I am still having an enema twice a week, which is both painful and awkward. When the male nurse comes to give me the enema, because he doesn't speak English, he enacts the whole process, making loud farting and shitting noises, as well as slapping his fists together so I can picture clearly what is going to take place.

He does this with some relish, and since he looks like Italian comedian Dario Fo, the whole performance seems hilarious, not least to him.

The following day, in a separate incident, a doctor visits me, presses my stomach and then, to make sure that all is working properly, sticks his finger up my arse. I now designate my arse Route 66. The female nurse, a friend, giggles, 'Hey, you might even start to enjoy this.'

Then she removes my catheter. This, apparently, is progress. Now every four hours a nurse presses a tube into the end of my penis which sucks out my urine. It is horrible at night, because when you are asleep, you might wake up to find a nurse with his hand around your balls.

Still, as Isabella says, enough already of

the shit and piss. Do they really want to hear it? But this is the reality of life here for most of the patients. For us, this hospital seems to encompass the entire universe. I cannot believe it when Isabella leaves to have dinner with her family or friends. There really is another world out there where people drink, laugh and finger one another with pleasure.

All this shrivelled-cock talk reminds me that I must finish the Amsterdam orgy story. There was a time when I was not in hospital and was even horny.

I am doing more physiotherapy to accelerate my recovery, which takes three hours a day, rendering me exhausted.

When I grew up, children were rarely praised or encouraged. The educational ethos of the time was punishment and reprimand; a stick rather than a carrot.

On my first day at secondary school, our form teacher slapped two sticks down on the desk and said, 'This is Little Willy and Big Willy. One or other of these will be coming for you if you don't mind your lip.' Immediately I defecated in my trousers, as did, I imagine, several others in the class. It was the beginning of *The Terror*.

My father encouraged me to succeed as a writer, but neither he nor my mother praised us. I don't remember many compliments for any of the other kids I knew in the school or in the neighbourhood. In fact I knew that many of the kids were kicked and punched by their parents. Approbation would do something called 'spoiling' children. Too much veneration would hold up their progress and they would deliquesce like an ice cream in the sun. This idea was not contested until the countercultural late 1960s, when the educational ethos began to change from punishment to gentle encouragement under the influence of educationalists like Donald Winnicott, Bruno Bettelheim, Anna Freud, Carl Rogers and others.

Children who had been traumatized by the war were finally addressed kindly, unlike children previously who were treated like a wild species who had to be beaten into respectability.

I am not one for the indiscriminate, neo-liberal fantasy of today, where young people are told that they can 'have it all' or 'be whatever they want to be'. This kind of cruel optimism and fatuous use of illusion and ideology is as useless as any punishment and leads the child nowhere.

My writing students are not children, and whether they are praised or unpraised is beside the point. My work as a teacher is neither to uplift nor discourage them, but to say something that will help them move on as writers. I want to help them say something tomorrow that they couldn't say yesterday.

But, if they do write something that brings a smile to my face, I will tell them. After all, the aim of so-called creative writing is to give pleasure, and if the students succeed in doing so, they should know it, because they are in show-biz. This writing work is not therapy for the writer but entertainment for the reader.

It is important when you are writing, or creating anything, to be aware of an audience. This may be one person, several, or a crowd. These others will orientate you, so when you are reading through your work, you will ask yourself if what you have done is clear, does it make sense, are the audience bored, are they still there, or have they left already?

For instance, the writer must be aware that a novel should get off to a good strong start, there shouldn't be pages of warm-up, of easing slowly into the narrative. It has to kick off compellingly. The story should have a certain pace, which will keep the reader at the book. When I am reading my students' work, what I look out for is an original point of view; someone who sees the world in a new and interesting way, a writer who wakes me up and makes me think: I never saw things like that before.

I am neither an art-for-art's-sake guy, nor am I a man who likes art to be purely commercial; the best artists, the ones I admire – Miles Davis, the Beatles, Hitchcock, etc. – are able to combine serious ideas within a commercial envelope.

Back to praise and criticism, it is odd that writers are more likely to believe the vile things that are sometimes said about their work, particularly by professional critics, than good things said by friends. There is no reason to believe that an unpleasant remark should carry more weight than a pleasant one. But who hasn't given false praise to friends? It is difficult to gauge the truthfulness of those closest to you. Quite rightly, they want to cheer us up.

Nevertheless, when you receive a reaction to your work from critics and friends, you should be able to measure the value of it, and whether your work has resonated with an audience at all.

If it has, you should be able to take this praise seriously and use the reaction as a charge for the future, to keep going. Unfortunately, we are afraid of being praised since it might give rise to envy in others, who might then hate us, or worse, be humiliated.

Work liberates us. We are making a contribution to the world; our art is for others and not for ourselves alone; a connection is being made. This is the spark of life, a kind of love. We should be able to enjoy our successes and love ourselves in proportion to them.

*

This afternoon I stood up for the first time since my accident. I was strapped to a gurney and raised up above my natural height, but in a standing position. I felt such a sense of exhilaration and pride I almost cheered myself. Perhaps at last I can afford a little optimism, and even praise.

14/02/2023

My father had been an enthusiastic and warm dad. He and his brothers and sisters, in a large Muslim family, loved having kids around – mind you, often with many servants to look after them. I was brought up at a time – the early post-war period – when men, or at least fathers, were bosses, patriarchs, heads of the family; women were mostly housewives, and children were supposed to be children. All this strict organization, and gender and generational differentiation, began to fall apart in the 1960s and 1970s.

There has barely been a minute of the last ten years when I haven't enjoyed being with my three sons, Sachin, Carlo and Kier. But I admit that the early days were difficult, if not nasty, and even hair-raising on occasion. I often felt I was in the wrong place, at the wrong time, with the wrong people, as if there were some other parallel world I was meant to be in. I am sure there isn't a parent in the world who wouldn't admit this. The people most likely to madden you are not those you merely hate, but those who raise the greatest, most insane-making conflicts in you. Freud refers to these strong alternating currents as ambivalence, which does not mean mixed feelings, but absolute hating and absolute loving, often at the same time.

My first two sons, Sachin and Carlo, are identical twins and, a bit like my accident, were a bomb dropped on me and my then partner, Tracey. I was in my late thirties and had always intended to become a parent. Somehow I never got round to it, though there had been a couple of near-misses. In the 1980s selfishness was the character ideal of the age, and fucking hell was it fun.

From the day I discovered Tracey was pregnant with twins, dadness, I found, was more catastrophic than marvellous, as people told me it usually is at the beginning, and even in the middle. I felt as I do about my accident: that something both irretrievable and disastrous had happened, and there was no going back.

Tracey and I had somehow stepped through

a mirror and walked into another world of instant insolvency, screaming midnights, nappies, and more nappies. I remember dragging the kids out of their cots at six o'clock one Sunday morning, getting them dressed on the living-room floor – already filthy with children's detritus – shoving them wailing into their pushchair, and heaving this huge unmanageable double-buggy up the hilly street and into Holland Park.

It must have been a rainy summer; still, I sat on the damp grass as the kids danced in a muddy puddle until they were black, while around me lay youthful, exhausted revellers, who had just fallen out of a club, and were coming down. That should have been me.

My first novel, *The Buddha of Suburbia*, had been published eighteen months or so before. I was researching and writing my second novel, *The Black Album*, which was to be about the nefarious effect of a nascent Islamic fundamentalism on a new generation of Asian kids, rebelling against what they saw as their more quiescent and cowed parents. I recognized at last I had to become a serious writer and earn a living from my pen until these little bastards were educated and almost grown up.

It took me a few years to start enjoying them, and along the way I found myself in many uncomfortable situations. I hated taking them to the various activities the times demanded, like karate, football and swimming, which involved wasting hours with the parents of other kids, whom I found utterly boring, particularly Simon's dad, a half-wit money manager.

I found myself shuffling about listlessly; I always wanted to be somewhere else, but where? Doing what? And when I wasn't serving the kids, I felt guilty as hell. But I had to get used to this and bear the guilt. I had spent many years doing what I wanted, when I wanted, and I guess I had spoiled myself, becoming entitled and arrogant.

I have to say, the kid-world, where you are just another inadequate parent, made me feel frustrated and alienated. Now I had to adjust to reality like everyone else, and I made a right sulky and miserable fuss over it.

Then I repeated the experience with my

third son, Kier. I had split up with Tracey when the twins were two years old. But this time I was determined to stick it out with Kier, with whose mother I remained until he was fifteen.

My beard has always grown quickly. In the hospital, I am shaved by Diego, a Lazio-supporting nurse who speaks little English, but who once saved my life following the incident with the fish, and of whom I am fond. We communicate through Google Translate and he tells me that his wife is reading *The Buddha of Suburbia*. But he is not always around, so now I have lassoed Sachin, who is currently visiting, into giving me a wet shave. It goes without saying that I am nervous of this sometime-clumsy kid coming at my neck with a razor. He wets my face, applies cream, and shaves me without mistake. He does a good job. Our positions are now reversed: he looks after me as I once looked after him, but with less complaint. It has worked out well.

27/02/2023

I am waiting for my hypnotist to call. He's been recommended by a friend; I went to him before, years ago when I had writer's block. It did actually work insofar as I was able to continue as a writer, fortunately or unfortunately for the public. Let's hope he has magical healing powers this time as well.

For the first couple of weeks after my accident, I was drugged and pretty much knocked out from the trauma, though I was writing, or thinking about writing, almost continuously.

It took me some time to get used to the utterly serious nature of my injury and how life-changing and permanent it is. There's no going back, though I wish all the time that there was.

I made friends almost immediately, tried to fit in, and get used to the institution. But the Maestro, whose company I found stimulating and uplifting, has become chronically ill with pneumonia and has been moved from this rehab to another hospital.

Since I have been in hospital, I haven't been able to drink, take illegal drugs, or smoke. I went cold turkey from the moment I was admitted, and I wonder if this has had an effect on my sleeping. Miss S has been coming to my room every morning, sharing her smart black vape with me. She introduced me to vaping, which I had never tried before, and it is a minor vice which I enjoy. You are allowed to vape in this hospital, and the nurses lift the cylinder to my mouth when they pass by. Miss S and I smoke, her putting the vape to my lips, as we have long conversations about our friends and families, time-passing discussions I would never have had in the ordinary course of things. But recently she has been suffering from pneumonia and could be depressed. I hardly see her now.

I've started to feel that I'm breaking down; the sheer tedium of being in the same room day and night, as others speak over me in a language I don't understand.

The constant medical interventions – whether for my own good or not – have begun to create in me a series of anxieties, fears and paranoias that I can't overcome.

My defences — good cheer and love of jokes — can't get me through this: the hospital smell, the despair, and the hatred of my condition, the constant realization that I am disabled. It has reduced me to a hopelessness I've never known in my life. I am experiencing a terrible Edgar Allan Poe feeling of being entombed in my own body.

I exist in a constant state of panic, fear and tearfulness. I want to escape myself.

Isabella, who's been here looking after me for most of the day, is suffering from exhaustion and anguish. This rupture has devastated her as well. We have minor arguments we've never had before, and must ensure don't become more entrenched. This accident has made me aggressive and angrier. I'm in a relentless rage, which isn't surprising. My twin sons and Tracey, their mother and my close friend, are also suffering from various anxiety symptoms.

My exit from this place, which I desire as soon as possible, presents numerous logistical problems. I can't just walk out. There's the issue of where I might go and the bureaucratic protocols that are required when moving hospital following a serious injury.

I've often wondered whether I'm quite an indecisive person. Sitting here alone in my wheelchair, I have plenty of time to reflect on how I have lived my life. I know there are many matters, times and occasions when I haven't taken action where it would have benefited me. I have been cautious and hysterically shilly-shallying at times, expecting less from the world than it might have given me had I shown more courage and been less afraid of what others might think.

At least my accident seems to have given me the impression that indecisiveness is not going to help me. I know for sure that I need to get out of here.

Sachin has been with me for the last two days and my mental state seems to have stabilized. I have spent most of my life in some form of isolation, since reading and writing, once my major preoccupations, one does alone. I enjoyed my own company, music and long walks. But that is not what I need now.

I still haven't heard from the hypnotist. Whatever. I am determined in my current writing to express exactly how I feel; this darkness is my truth.

My hope is to get out of here and return to London where at least I'll be in a more familiar environment, and have friends nearby who might visit. What I need is distraction and companionship. The worst part of the day is the early evening when Isabella puts on her coat and leaves. When I see her walk out of the door, I know I have to survive the night without her, alone.

05/03/2023

I was lucky in my mid-teens to discover writing and literature, pornography and drugs, around the same time. My working day would begin in earnest at 4.30 p.m. when I arrived home from school, sat at the typewriter my father had given me, put on a record or turned on the radio, and resumed work on the novel I was writing about someone like me slowly drowning in misery at school. I knew at least that writing had to be my ticket into the funkier world that existed an hour away, 'up London'.

The literature I was reading might be described as hard: Russian, British, French classics from my dad's library (if I didn't educate myself, no one else was going to). But the drugs and pornography available to us were soft by contemporary standards.

The newspapers might say the country was awash with drugs, but I can't tell you how difficult it was to obtain a bit of crumbly brown hash. We would score at college gigs, or from hippy friends in pubs like Henekey's on Bromley High Street or the famous Three Tuns in Beckenham, where there was live music in the back room. There is a famous picture of David Bowie playing there, with what looks like a perm, perched on a plinth strumming an acoustic guitar.

We would attempt to get high on this terrible brown shit – it was commonly referred to as 'shit' – and go to see the Faces or Pink Floyd at Crystal Palace Bowl.

It wasn't until I started taking speed, blue pills called Blues, that I saw both how effective and enjoyable drugs could be and what a deleterious effect they could have on your mind.

Man, those Blues were depressing when you came down from them.

The most exciting drug in those days, and the one we all enjoyed the most, was LSD. It was cheap and we would take a lot of it – at parties, concerts and even at home when times got slow.

As for porn, it was difficult in the mid-1960s to see an image of a naked woman save in an Impressionist painting. The magazines we could get our hands on, which were passed around, displayed female breasts but the vaginas were air-brushed and flat.

My first enjoyable experience of pornography was in books. My father had many of the sexually experimental titles, *Lady Chatterley's Lover*, *Lolita* and even *Ulysses*.

The most overtly pornographic novel at that time, was by for me the most entertaining writer – and one I still love to this day – Henry Miller. *The Tropic of Cancer* and Miller's great trilogy, *Sexus*, *Plexus* and *Nexus*, provided both the great thrill of writing with interludes of pornography which you could cheerfully masturbate to.

At school these were called 'one-hand reads'; some of the pages got sticky and yellow. It must seem odd now to think if you wanted a wank you'd read a book. But for a young, inexperienced kid like myself, some of these books – particularly the Victorian pornographic ones, like *The Pearl* – were a revelation. When I read about cunnilingus and fellatio for the first time, I was appalled and amazed that anyone would want to put their lips against somebody else's genitalia.

Victorian pornography also featured

dungeons, whipping and other forms of what is now called BDSM. I was, to say the least, blown away by the possibility of what my life might look like if I could get over my nerves and find a dungeon. These stories were advertisements for the future.

I read *The Story of O*, as well as Georges Bataille's *Story of the Eye*, and was shaken by how literature and extreme sexuality could be so powerful and effective. As Sachin recently said, these stories are more than an adolescent's imagination could conjure themselves. They draw you into a world of filth and depravity – which will remain rewarding throughout your life – reminding you how close sexuality and disgust have to be for sex to retain its edge. But if you really wanted to learn about sexuality, as opposed to the conventions of courtship and marriage, you couldn't go to literature. Literature was censored and self-censored – I would have loved to have known what George Eliot thought about anal sex. Why did Swann love fucking Odette so much; what was it about her voice or pussy that made him decide to throw

away his life? Great literature was never explicit enough.

It was in the mid-1970s, when I was in my
early twenties, that I began to write pornography for a living, just a few articles for the
flourishing top-shelf magazine market of the
time, mostly sold in Asian corner shops. I also
wrote serious articles about Aubrey Beardsley
and the Marquis de Sade for semi-serious porn
magazines like *Mayfair*.

It is not easy to write porn. How do you
describe an erect penis or an orgasm? Clichés come easily; words like 'throbbing' and
'enormous' are difficult to avoid. All writing
is demanding but finding new language for the
sexual act is almost impossible, particularly when
I was being paid around twelve pounds per article.

The best way to write about sexuality is to
describe its meaning for the participants. But
with magazine porn, the reader doesn't want
a Lacanian disquisition on desire, just an erec-
tion. It's a banal form.

While I was writing these little porny stories, my close friend the Leather and I decided

that we would become gigolos. We would hang around outside Harrods in our best clothes hoping to be picked up by rich women who would reward us for the sexual pleasures we would lavish on them. Luckily for us, and even luckier for the women, we didn't get any offers except from a couple of old queens, whom we were too coy to go with.

During this punk period, performance artists like Cosey Fanni Tutti exposed themselves in porn magazines as forms of artistic expression. They wanted to outrage, but this also had the effect of bringing obscure pornographic paraphernalia into the mainstream. At the far end of the King's Road, in a funny little curiosity of a shop, Vivienne Westwood and Malcolm McLaren were bringing formerly secretive porn clothes made from rubber and leather into pubs, clubs and the high street.

Sex can make us lose our minds. Every day a pop star, politician or industrialist does something carnal guaranteed to ruin their lives.

Who hasn't at some time engaged in filthily risky behaviour for the sake of a fantasy or

an orgasm? At the end of the nineteenth cen-
tury, Freud theorized that fantasy and extreme
sexuality are at the centre of our culture. For
some of us, fantasy and masturbation are the
most exciting thing, if not the most fulfilling,
thing in our lives. Pornography and technology,
advance together. In my lifetime, visual pornography has metamorphosized from crude,
badly lit photographs – and what were called
'blue movies' – to VR headsets, anthropo-
morphic sex dolls and AI deepfakes.

All of this produces an ethical dilemma,
since real sex inevitably involves at least some
conversation and negotiation with the other;
and there is always the peril of rejection, failure
and humiliation. It is difficult to fail at a wank.
People are worried that porn and masturbating
will replace sex entirely, or that they are more
enjoyable.

As attitudes have liberalized, the drugs that
I've liked best have become more sophisticated.
I've had some great cocaine nights with my children, and I know friends who take MDMA with
their kids, though this isn't something I would do,

out of the fear of revealing too much. My boys did, though, introduce me to magic mushrooms.

Sex and drugs go together, like wine and a good meal. The idea isn't that people should be traumatized by sex, or drugs, but that they should be taught to love them, as essential pleasures.

But the age of liberalism is over. We have entered a new era of censorship and self-censorship. Both liberals and conservatives have become insistent on certain things not being said or heard. There is a terror of offence being given and offence taken.

The new pleasures afforded by technology have created a fear in the population of over-excitement and lack of control. And sometimes sexuality can become degraded in an attempt to render it worthless, mechanical and functional, rather than something that is essential to the human experience.

Unfortunately, the fight for freedoms gained since the 1960s has to be fought repeatedly. Sometimes it can feel like we've gone into reverse.

13/03/2023

The elegant Lady G visits me in bed most mornings with a cappuccino and cheerful gossip. She is an acquaintance of Isabella and a distinguished research doctor at this clinic, where she works in a lab, and is therefore allowed to see me outside visiting hours. She speaks perfect English, is generous and sophisticated – a European in the best sense – and is someone I would never have met otherwise.

She tells me a lovely story about a friend who became paralysed and could only communicate by winking. One morning, the woman became agitated and Lady G worried she was having a heart attack. With the use of an alphabet board, the woman was able to explain that she had an itch on her nose that needed scratching.

This story was particularly poignant for me because, as I am unable to use my hands, I cannot scratch myself either. Indeed, as I write this, I can feel a particularly virulent itch developing above my right ear, which is spreading across my head the more I think about it.

Getting yourself scratched is quite a procedure. You have to ask somebody to do it, and, if they are willing, they have to find the exact spot and provide the right amount of pressure – not too much, not too little. You can only ask them to do this so many times before you fear them becoming irritated. But some itches are in difficult spots: inside the ear or around your balls.

If you look at real people on television or examine others in a café, you will notice how often they touch their face. They are constantly caressing their eyes, pulling their nose or rubbing their cheeks. It is only now I realize what a luxury and a pleasure it is to scratch yourself.

It is sensual, reassuring, sexy; it can be ecstatic. The surface of the body is alive. Recently, when I allowed my beard to grow for more than three days, the surface of my face became rabidly irritated and I desperately needed to have it scratched. Isabella cooperated from time to time. It was a profound bliss to have her scratch me under the chin. I understand how lucky our dog, Cairo, is since his family and indeed strangers on the street rub, tickle and stroke him constantly. I am jealous; I envy my dog.

There are strict rules with regard to which parts of the body you can touch or scratch in social situations. You can feel your face and even your hair but not your arse, teeth or pubic region. The rules are different on beaches and in restaurants; they are also different for men and women. Children must be taught which bits of themselves it is legitimate to touch, and where and when. It is complicated and somewhat arbitrary.

As a substitute for their bodies, people are constantly playing with their phones. In the 1960s and 70s, I remember people fiddled with cigarettes, lighters, matches and even pipes. It gave them something to do with their hands while having conversations. Now people look at their phones, and even send texts during conversation. These distractions, far from being only an annoyance, are an outlet for anxiety; they help communication, creating a distance between you and the other person. You want to be close to someone but not too close.

Freud realized how difficult it was to sit face-to-face with a patient for eight hours a day. Being looked at, if not examined, for such a long time made him uncomfortable. Therefore he created the couch situation for psychoanalysis. This distance — the patient on their back — also enabled the patient to dream and free-associate within the session, and not try to keep the analyst amused or entertained.

I can't play with my phone; I can't blow my nose or rub my eyes. My hands move a little but they feel as though concrete has been poured into them. They are stiff and unmalleable; they won't do what my brain wants them to do, though they have started to move a bit after hours of physiotherapy. I still can't do anything useful with them.

The whole thing is a terrible loss and means I am entirely dependent on the goodwill of others. Fortunately, I have discovered that others do have plenty of generosity and patience. They are keen to do things for you if you ask them, and they often volunteer.

My injury has stimulated a different kind of love in people, and a desire in them to be useful in new ways. I can see what a pleasure it is for others to help me, and how much satisfaction it brings them. It has been an illuminating discovery, although this form of care doesn't feel like an equal one. Others are doing things for me and I cannot reciprocate – except with gratitude. It seems like a feeble exchange. But it matters.

As babies our first form of exchange is that of being loved. We are kissed and caressed, gurgled at and appreciated. We are loved into the world and even as we age we expect love from others as an initial impulse. We don't expect to be harmed, and if we are, we are shocked. As we get older we may become suspicious, afraid and disillusioned, but the expectation of love is never erased.

19/03/2023

If it hasn't been difficult enough, I have been told I am to move room again. It will be the third room I have shared since arriving here in mid-January. All the rooms are identical: painted light blue, with low ceilings and two beds side by side about six feet apart.

The room-mates change each time, which is a bit of a strain. Each transition is an abrupt and jarring alteration; Isabella and I are asked to gather up the numerous bits and pieces we've accumulated — food, electronic equipment, clothes, bedding, toiletries — and relocate within an hour. This time, I have the good fortune to be sharing a room with the Maestro, who has returned to the clinic after a spell in a general hospital.

I've been increasingly panicky and nervous over the last week. I have had a buzzing in my ears, a hot feeling throughout my body, and a terror that I am going to faint again, as I did on that terrible day of my accident. I am scared and fear things are getting out of control. My body feels as if it wants to shut down.

Despite being here for three months, I don't seem to have calmed down. Each day is relatively similar to the previous one, so it is possible to form a defensive ring of habit, but my barricades seem as weak now as at any time. I worry and am afraid for the future. If the definition of trauma is that of a devastating unexpected event which is impossible to psychically organize, then I have been subject to too many shocks recently. I am scared when I am separated from Isabella; I hate to be alone.

Every day we are subject to new experiences which need to be assimilated. The changes here – while not cruel – have been disorientating. Routine creates a buffer around us, nullifying the abrupt shocks and alterations of daily life, which is why people remain in situations that seem uncomfortable, if not quite wrong, for them. Familiarity gives our lives a comforting shape and form. My world here does have some repetition and domestic structure, but it is not a comfortable one.

Isabella's presence and words create reliability. But in some ways I have become an infant again, having been an adult for a time. I had agency once, a glimpse of some freedom, before it was withdrawn, leaving only dependence and the rage of helplessness.

At least with Isabella I have recognition. She knows who I am and why I suffer; I know the same about her. This idea of mutual recognition, of shared understanding – a kind of mirroring – is one of the reasons I started writing in the first place. I remember as a teenager wanting to write stories and novels because I thought that someone out there would recognize me and would understand what I was going through. Although I grasp the idea that stories are fundamentally entertainment, I see them not only as the most sophisticated form of fun, but as an attempt to communicate something about suffering.

But some traumas are excitements. Sexuality, for one thing, particularly for the young, is a mixture of fear and elation. There is a sense in all sexuality of wondering whether one can survive it and indeed take pleasure from it. You have to learn to endure your pleasures as well as your pains. If you can overcome your traumas, and indeed learn from them, then you might feel a sense of triumph.

What I am experiencing in this clinic has been an affront to my happiness and complacency, to my sense that the world was basically okay, the right way round. I can't help getting annoyed by the indignity, if not the stupidity, of what has happened to me, a mixture of tragedy and farce, which is the essence of Kafka's great absurdist work *The Trial*, or indeed all of his work.

My physio Fabio, whom Isabella and I refer to as James Bond since he looks like a romantic lead in a movie, is a sensitive, wise and Zen-like character. He has little English, I have no Italian, and I have to hand myself over to him, which I am happy to do because he is confident and strong. You can tell a lot from the way a physio touches you, if they seem secure and know what they are doing. Some others — and I have had several — are more tentative, and their work doesn't progress you. But Fabio has a plan.

Slowly he has me standing, first on a vertical bed, where I am strapped to a gurney and rise up, Christ-like, above the gym. It is euphoric to be so tall; and I manage it at first for five minutes, and then ten, and then for fifteen before I begin to feel dizzy and nauseous.

Next session he puts me on to another machine with a seat under my arse, which pushes me up into a standing position. This time, unlike with the gurney, I am not so high. It is more like a normal standing height. I can manage standing for ten minutes, or maybe a little longer, then the gym swims before my eyes and I need to lie down.

I am puzzled as to why doing a simple thing like standing up should have become so difficult and, at times, unendurable. But if you haven't stood up since Boxing Day last year, it becomes a dazzlingly complicated achievement, and one I am improving at.

On the second machine, with the seat under my arse, Miss S insists on accompanying me;

she smiles and yells encouragement from her chair. She is not surprised by how scared I am. It is normal to feel so vertiginous.

Next, Fabio is preparing me for a robot-like machine called the Lokomat, which helps those with spinal injuries to walk again. You are encased and suspended within this mechanism, which cradles your torso and limbs, moving them electronically.

I am afraid of this machine, that it will be like being locked into a suit of heavy armour. I could become claustrophobic as well as nauseous, embarrassing myself by freaking out. I am Fabio's challenge, because right now I am refusing to be put in the Lokomat. But the Lokomat *will* be my next step. I'm looking forward to it, and I am not looking forward to it.

02/04/2023

Nothing much to report since last time. Stuck in the interminable hell of hospital. A mixture of boredom and distress. Many fruitful and fruitless discussions with Isabella about whether I should stay here and make use of the good physiotherapy and get as strong and well as I can, or whether we should start making our way back to London where Isabella will have to live alone in my house while I am placed in a new rehab hospital.

I miss my city and my friends. The kids come and visit me every weekend. A good friend has just flown from London for lunch and then went straight back home; another English friend, who lives locally, has passed by and told me I appear the same as I was before, except that I can't walk or use my hands. Although Isabella is here all day and without her support I would be in deep shit, I still feel the need to see more people. Mainly as a distraction from my dark mood and situation, but also to keep in touch with the outside world, which has moved on without me, as if I were already dead. Being in hospital is like being in a time capsule. I am getting too morbid and require cheering up.

I thought I would finish the Amsterdam orgy story. It is being typed not by Isabella but by my youngest son, Kier, who is twenty-four. He is a little freaked by the idea of writing this down but here goes anyway:

Iris came into the hotel room with her boyfriend, who was younger than me but not that much younger. He was around forty and seemed to be the same size as I am – not tall and a bit stocky – but shabbier, with dishevelled grey hair and a beard. I think his name was Hans.

He didn't speak much English but the three of us sat at the table, smoked a joint, and chatted in a desultory way. The excitement I had felt earlier had disappeared and I was at a loss as to what to do or say. I wondered if the orgy idea was dead and we would end up going out to dinner or something equally dull. Fortunately Iris stood up and said she was keen that we get on with it. She had done what I requested, which was to bring a friend round for a threesome, and that was what we were going to do.

She took off her clothes and I quickly did the same, thinking, fuck it, why lose this opportunity to have some fun? She and I got on the bed and started to make out.

Hans was still wearing his long black overcoat which, to my surprise, he didn't remove. Iris explained to me, as we started to have sex, that Hans liked to watch. She asked me if I minded but what could I say? So, while she and I energetically fucked, he sat on the end of the bed observing. I couldn't help glancing up at this enigmatic figure, saying nothing and showing no emotion. She asked him if he wanted to join in but to my relief he shook his head.

At one point Iris and I decided we were hungry so Hans ordered some food. When room service arrived, Hans held up a blanket to cover us while the waiter pushed in the food trolley. Hans sat there gloomily watching his naked girlfriend eat sushi with another man. Perhaps this was some kind of punishment or masochistic kink. But if this was his thing, he didn't seem to enjoy it. My impression was that they hadn't done this before.

After a couple of hours, Iris got dressed and the two of them left. I opened the window, looked out at the city and smoked another joint. I had had a great and memorable – if not weird – time and was keen to see Iris again since she was coming to London.

A few weeks later, Iris and I arranged to meet in the Portobello Road. I had taken Kier to school in the morning and Iris and I were going to see each other at lunchtime. I wanted to ask her what exactly had happened with Hans in Amsterdam. I wondered if they were still together.

But that day London was in chaos. The Tube had stopped and the buses weren't running. People on the street said there had been a power outage and the city had shut down. Others were saying some kind of atrocity had taken place but nobody knew the details. Then I saw people sitting on benches looking devastated. The area resounded with police, ambulance and fire engine sirens. The date was 7 July 2005, which became notorious for the '7/7' bombings. Fifty-two people were killed in four separate suicide attacks. Iris and I didn't manage to meet up and I never saw her again.

09/04/2023

Earlier this week, David of Bromley flew from Canada to visit me for four days. Staying in central Rome, he took the bus out to the hospital, and sat with me through the lunch that Isabella always brings me. He pushed me around Santa Lucia's open green space — each inch of which I now know, every bump and blade of grass — while we discussed whatever came into our minds, from childhood to ageing, children, our parents, and in particular, life in Beckenham and Bromley in the 1970s.

Although David is the same age as me, he was in the year above at school. He was the classic heart-throb and cool kid, with hair down to his shoulders. The headmaster called his bell-bottoms 'sailor's trousers' and referred to him as 'girlie'. David knew the young David Bowie from the Three Tuns pub, who was then living with Angie, his exciting American girlfriend, in nearby Haddon Hall. David of Bromley brought early Pink Floyd and King Crimson albums to my house in the evenings. Sitting downstairs in our tiny living room with my father, David delighted Dad with his attention, giving him the opportunity to discuss his favourite subject, Eastern religion, and what Zen could teach the West about what he called 'spiritual values'. Dad believed the West was becoming materialistic and was forgetting to ask the most important questions about the meaning and value of living. David would listen like an enthralled disciple.

My father was a friend of David's mother, who was considered sexy and refined by David's hippy friends and me. It was said in school that when David was in bed with his girlfriend his mum would bring them breakfast, before shooing them off to class.

The opening chapter of *The Buddha of Suburbia* centres on the naive seventeen-year-old hero, Karim Amir, along with his father, an Indian immigrant from Bombay, now working as a civil servant. One evening they go to Beckenham – a suburb posher than the one Karim's family live in – to visit Charlie, Karim's schoolfriend and hero. The father has been invited by Eva Kay, Charlie's mother, to present a yoga class and talk to the assembled white suburbanites about Zen Buddhism.

During the course of this eventful evening, Karim finds his father and Eva having sex on a bench in the garden. Shocked, he flees upstairs to Charlie's bedroom — a cool cave in the attic, adorned with pictures of the Beatles during their Sergeant Pepper period — where he masturbates a stoned Charlie. It is Karim's first homosexual experience.

This first chapter was originally a short story. On a flight to Canada, I had nothing to read but I had my ever-present notebook, where I wrote the entire thing in nine hours, from London to Quebec. It was published in the *London Review of Books* and later, having always wanted to write a novel, I returned to it and built the narrative around this opening.

Little of this audacious suburban scenario actually took place. I do remember going excitedly to David's house one evening with my father, his mother playing Bach. But now, this chapter of the book, and my reimagining of the scene, has replaced any real memory of the event. I guess this is how memory and fiction work together: there was an initial scene, which is copied and elaborated, inflected with fantasy and desire, until it becomes something else entirely.

Charlie, or Charlie Hero as he becomes, is nothing like the real David, with whom I lost contact after school, but reconnected with later. Charlie Hero was based on other boys I knew in the punk scene, including what was known as the 'Bromley Contingent', made up of my school friends. But he really became himself because of the demands of the novel. Karim remains in love with him, and continues to idolize him, even as Charlie becomes wilder and crueller. David himself, though once a wild person, was never unkind, and was always vulnerable, interesting and sweet.

Sachin, who is typing this, tells me about a fifteen-year-old kid he idolized at school who would scrawl tattoos on his arms in pen, carried a guitar on his back, and had spiky hair, defying the rules.

Girls and boys alike do this veneration and identification. It is an important stage of childhood, when who we want to be is embodied in another person, an ideal self and paragon, whom we are narcissistically in love with.

We make ourselves out of others, particularly at this age. They are our social and sexual templates. Our idols are apparently immune from pubertal terrors, fears and social awkwardness, as well as the physical disfigurement of that period between childhood and adulthood, which we all have to endure. Do we ever idealize others like we did when we were at school?

16/04/2023

My father spent his working life as a civil servant in the Pakistani Embassy in London. Occasionally he wrote sports journalism for Indian and Pakistani newspapers, covering squash and cricket. Primarily he wanted to be a novelist, and believed this was a skill you might learn from books. He became an enthusiastic reader of writing manuals, though there were far fewer then than there are now. But they did include classics like Dorothea Brande's *Becoming a Writer* and Ray Bradbury's *Zen in the Art of Writing*. Because Dad liked to talk about these books and what he would call 'the whole technique of writing', I would read them as well, trying to pick up tips. I've continued to read and collect these writing guides and have several shelves of them at home. They are a good way to avoid getting down to actual writing. Several of my favourites are the many volumes of the *Paris Review* interviews, which are among the most honest and realistic pictures of what it really is to suffer the agonies and pleasures of being a working writer.

These books were published before the word 'creative' was regularly added to the word 'writing'. I'd like to find out when this fatuous redundancy became common, and I could clout the culprit over the head.

The latest so-called creative writing books – of which I have read several, and even been quoted in some – are, in keeping with our neo-liberal times, more prescriptive and dogmatic in terms of form and structure than the ones I grew up with. Mostly written with film and television in mind, they tell you where and when there should be a conflict or a climax, and often at which page. This kind of formulaic patterning is more like colouring-in than real writing. It's certainly not creative but the idea is to get television shows off the ground rather than produce interesting, original work.

From Shakespeare to *Hollyoaks*, all writing manuals talk about the necessity of conflict driving each scene: between individuals, classes, races, countries, neighbours or whatever. It would be strange, experimental and interesting — like an absurdist drama – to write a play or movie in which the characters were only nice to one another, exchanged gifts, said flattering things, had wonderful sex, and then resolved all wars by shaking hands and hugging. It would resemble a movie made up entirely of happy endings.

I have been in hospital since December and as we enter the fresh Roman spring – probably the most pleasant Italian season; it is not yet too hot – I have had more and more visitors. Many friends have started to look in on me, coming from all over the world. Others have been passing through Rome, and have popped in to see me at lunchtime. Far from being conflictual, argumentative and difficult, these conversations are entertaining and informational, full of fun and giggles, helping me forget myself.

But I do wonder – I can't help it – about how others see me, now I am crippled. Do they look at me and find me abhorrent? Do they pity me? Do they love me more, less, or the same amount? Have I become some kind of love-test for them? Will they want to come and see me again? Or will they feel they have done their duty? What emotions do I arouse in others?

Sometimes I feel ashamed and humiliated by what has happened to me. I can't help wondering if somehow it's my fault. But these are morbid thoughts. Mostly my illness draws out the best in others and seems to have done the same to me. These generous friends always bring gifts. They are curious, they listen and they want to hear about how I'm doing. I have had visits from close friends, acquaintances, and people I barely know. Semi-strangers write asking if they may visit. I always say yes.

Isabella says that I like to complain about being isolated, abandoned and lonely, but my daily diary is full; I can hardly fit everyone in. Sometimes people have to overlap. In London, before my accident, I barely saw anyone apart from family, but now I have become what one friend described as a 'social butterfly'.

You would think from reading any drama that the world is full of terror, terrible marriages, bad sex and wars. And it is true that I myself have been the subject of a catastrophe, but this is nothing like the whole story which, if it is to be the whole story, will have to include stretches of harmony, joy, and the pleasure that people can take in one another's company. How much people want to give one another; how altruistic they can be. Gentleness and kindness — it's hardly dramatic, but there's a lot of it about.

29/04/2023

I've been here in Santa Lucia since January 14th, too long. My sanity, such as it is, is being tested. Unfortunately I've been unable to go mad; it is not something you can wish on yourself. I'm desperate to escape. More than anything I want to get out and return to London, though London is probably something of a fantasy. I like to imagine things will be better once I am in my home city, back with my friends and family, but I also know that might not necessarily be the case. Things will inevitably continue to be difficult.

I am afraid of leaving here. I am afraid of staying here. The boredom is overwhelming. I am having less physiotherapy than before; the course I was on has come to an end, which means I am lying in my bed for hours with little to do.

It is difficult for me to read. I've sort of figured out how to scan the newspapers using voice control. A friendly paraplegic from Milan sent me a MacBook Air which I can use with the help of Siri. It is hard work yelling at a computer, and it is not always so efficient. I listen to audio-books, but my situation sours them, rendering them morbid by my gloomy state of mind.

The Maestro has left my room; he has pneumonia again and has been moved to a general hospital for serious treatment. Miss S is leaving next week, to a flat in Rome. Since my significant friends here have gone, I feel left behind. I'm trying to move to a hospital in London, but it's proving to be complicated and slow because I have to enter through the British NHS system. I have to be assessed at a general hospital before moving to a specialist rehab facility outside London.

I'm using the Lokomat regularly, I've overcome my fear of the walking machine, and have been told I am making progress. My dizziness has gone. It's wonderful to have the illusion of motion again, and as I 'walk' for about thirty minutes at a time, I imagine I am striding alongside the river at Hammersmith with our dog, Cairo. I miss the ordinary things and wonder whether I can get back to them.

I talk on the phone to my analyst once a week. I've been in conversation with him for almost thirty years, and he continues to say fresh things that surprise and stimulate me. It's a unique relationship: I've spent more time talking with him than I ever did with my parents, and talk more intimately with him than I do with my friends. Some of my writing has come out of our conversations, and when I was lying on his couch, during the useful silences, I would have many ideas. Once I asked if his other patients, some of them writers, talked about their work. He said most of them didn't, they had other issues.

Carlo arrived yesterday and shaved me, as Sachin did last week. We walked around the garden and talked; I love to hear about their lives and what they're doing. It also gives Isabella a break. It's horrible to be helpless; losing the use of my hands is the worst thing that's happened to me. I pray that I will have more movement in the future, or at least in one hand.

30/04/2023

It's the morning and I am chatting to Lady G, who has brought me pasticcini and cappuccino. She and I have long conversations about family issues, serious talk about AI and politics, and anything else that crosses our minds. Today we are talking about vocation. Once, while teaching a clever student, she made the mistake of asking him why he wanted to be a nurse rather than a doctor. The question was offensive; it never occurred to him to be a doctor; being a nurse wasn't to be a failed doctor. It was a vocation in itself. As a child, a nurse helped his sick mother, and from that moment he knew what he wanted to do. Nothing would deflect him.

In every town, in every city in the world, there are hospitals that are full of nurses doing a devoted job. From the conversations I've had with the nurses, with whom I spend most of my days, and some of my nights – not having known any before – they consider their work to be a vocation, a calling, a whole way of life. They dress and undress me, wash my body, genitals and arse, cleaning everything. They brush my hair, change my dressings, feed and engage me in conversations; insert suppositories, change my catheter and brush my teeth, shave and transfer me from bed to chair – this is their everyday work. They are well trained and skilled, adept with complex medical equipment; it is technical labour, not an easy job.

The nurses here are cheerful, they sing and make jokes, but they are not well paid. Wages are certainly lower in Italy than they are in the UK but they have been doing this for years and, as far as I can tell, want to carry on. One nurse told me he didn't have a girlfriend because he was too exhausted from his work to sustain a romantic relationship. His favourite TV shows were set in hospitals; he liked anything that involved whole populations being wiped out by fatal diseases.

I am phobic about strangers' bodies. I wouldn't want to inject them, give them pills, turn them over, clip their fingernails and wash them. Do I have anything in common with these nurses? How can I understand them?

There is also a sexual aspect to the notion of vocation, since such a choice, like sexuality, isn't an option, but something you are inexorably drawn to. It chooses you, rather than the other way round. As with sexuality, such a mission is like a perversion; something you cannot live without and compulsively act on. I cannot be persuaded out of my desire to write. It is at the centre of my being.

The daily rituals of professional writers have always fascinated me. How much time they spend at their desk, whether they use a fountain pen or typewriter, and how many words or pages they like to do a day. Trivial stuff, but not to me.

Recently I was reading about a very successful writer. (I should add here that Isabella was reading the article to me, since I can no longer use my hands or pick up a book or magazine, but I am fortunate to love her voice and accent.) This writer in question produces two novels a year. He spends around ten hours a day writing and has produced about a hundred and thirty books.

This is a level of obsession that I do not envy and would never aspire to. I have always been able to go whole days without writing — often having better, more interesting things to do — and sometimes I wonder whether it would be self-destructive, or liberating, to stop completely. In truth, I have never gone more than a week without writing something. When I finally get down to it, I am amazed by how naturally it comes to me. But it never stops making me anxious.

After Isabella read me the piece about the obsessional writer who once went on a 36-hour writing jag, she read me another piece, still from the excellent website *Arts and Letters*, about the Japanese writer Haruki Murakami. He has his own form of obsessionality, which he describes in his essay collection *Novelist as a Vocation*. Apparently, he never goes a day without completing sixteen hundred words. That is a lot. I consider myself lucky if I produce a thousand words a week.

I thought about this, worrying that I was lazy. There was no way I could compete with Murakami. Anyway, I decided, the number of words one completes is irrelevant. It would be like an architect wanting to make sure he's laid two thousand bricks in one day. It is the idea, the shape and the force of the piece which matters.

Writing can be used – sitting alone in a room, typing – as a refuge, a hiding place. You are concealing yourself from others and the world, living entirely in your own mind. But it might be useful to remind yourself that there could be more nourishing places to be than in one's own imagination.

I like to think about what the writing of others has meant to me and still does; what a strange world we would live in without stories, novels, journalism, blogs, TV shows and cinema. Writers nurse the human soul through its difficult journey in this impossible life.

Teaching is an adjunct to writing. I began to teach writing when I first worked at the Royal Court Theatre in my early twenties, and I have taught ever since. I often wonder, as I guess most teachers do, whether I am doing anyone any good. But I enjoy it. I like to talk about structure, organization, voice, agents, publishers and TV shows. I'm interested in the lives of my students, and I'm happy when they progress. I admit that sometimes it is difficult to read their stuff. Real talent is rare and surprising; it is a gift, which must be elevated with discipline, and cannot be purchased on a course. Oddly, the writers themselves are usually more interesting than their work. But teaching is a calling too, and it feels necessary. After a fruitful session, I feel I've done something useful and helped someone as I have been bettered by good editors and astute readers who know how to talk about writing.

Good news and bad news. The good stuff is that Miss S, with her glorious two-toned hair, has finally, after some delay, gone home having spent six months in here, though she will return to swim and use the gym. The bad news is that the Maestro, with whom I was happy to share a room, has died in another hospital. Isabella went to his funeral and I was sorry not to be able to attend. He was a talented and sweet man, and a good friend. His partner and his two daughters will miss him.

Isabella and I are still trying to get back to London. It is time. I've been in the same place, virtually the same room, along with Isabella, for four months and I'm surprised not to be madder than I am. Certainly we are both worn out.

16/05/2023

Earlier this week I had the good fortune to be visited by an ex-student who was brought up in Nigeria and has been working on a novel set there. I've only read the beginning of the book and have been unable to continue. (I haven't yet figured out how to scroll down through documents without Isabella.) Anyhow, when the student had written a considerable amount of the book, she decided to show it not to an editor, friend, publisher or agent, but to a so-called 'sensitivity reader'. She was concerned about whether her work would be politically correct, and whether the book would get past an agent, let alone to a publisher. This is a trend I've noticed with other students and also with editors at publishing houses: whether a writer's work will be condemned for sexism, racism, cultural appropriation, and so on. It has become one of the main anxieties for young writers today.

Another student of mine wrote a good thriller from the point of view of a promiscuous

American lesbian and was thoroughly criticized by his tutor. How could he imagine for a moment that he was American, let alone a lesbian? The writer then got himself into a terrible tangle about who can write what and from which perspective. He rewrote the book and made it much worse, having been made to believe he was committing a literary crime by entering the mind of someone other than himself.

Some people are censorial, excited, if not turned on, by controlling others' speech and freedoms. There is an element of the left which is bursting with aggressive self-righteousness and self-defeating puritanism. The writers I prefer, the ones I grew up with, are the wild ones, the demented, the rude ones who don't give a damn. Dostoevsky, Plath, Rhys, Céline, Burroughs, Miller, Baldwin. I could add many more and it would be a list of some of our greatest and most admired artists. They wrote without fear or inhibition, and many have been prosecuted and condemned. Think of what the great Salman Rushdie has been through in the name of satire and criticism of authority.

The fatwa, in February 1989, was the first time I was aware that there could be real-life consequences for attacking tyrannous institutions and regimes through literature. After that, I know there were writers who were afraid to speak freely about the politicized version of Islam, or even about Muslims in general. It is worse now than ever before.

It is part of the writer's job to be offensive, to blaspheme, to outrage and even to insult. As Kafka says in one of his notebooks: 'Art should be an axe to smash the sea frozen inside us.' Culture should not be safe or complacent, and should frighten, if not alarm. It is the work of writers to turn the world upside down, to present opinions which go against prevailing trends. It is not our job to please but to challenge, to make us think differently about our bodies, our sexuality, politics and normativity.

What would a 'sensitivity reader' have made of the work of D. H. Lawrence or William Burroughs? One of the things I've noticed about my students is that they are already constrained.

When I began working on *The Buddha of*

Suburbia, I was determined to write it with as much disinhibition and freedom as I could. I would make it dirty and funny, not holding back or hesitating to say anything I truly felt. I didn't set out to shock, but to tell the story in the most candid way.

Before this, in 1984, working on the script of *My Beautiful Laundrette*, Stephen Frears, the director, who is not keen on script development, gave me one note: to make it 'dirtier, outrageous and more shocking'. His remarks were freeing, and I felt the script to be the first thing I had written in my own voice. I wonder, with these early works of mine – *My Beautiful Laundrette*, *Sammy and Rosie Get Laid*, *The Black Album* and *Intimacy* – what a 'sensitivity reader' would have made of them and what butchery would have gone on; whether I would even have a career now. I am relieved not to be a young writer today, working in this atmosphere of self-consciousness and trepidation, this North Korea of the mind.

The Buddha of Suburbia is full of racial insults and lewd, politically incorrect language, being written from the point of view of a dirty-minded seventeen-year-old mixed-race kid.

Kier, who is here with me now, and works in a school, informs me of what a stifling environment of fear and apprehension he lives in when it comes to speaking and creativity.

We should not forget that the insult can be an indication of friendship and admiration; we sometimes call one another 'cunts' and 'arse-holes' out of fondness rather than cruelty.

This over-corrected behaviour has been created by the right to make us lefties and liberals seem foolish and petty with our silly disputes about language and point of view. The work of us in political opposition is not to fight among ourselves but to create a world in which there is no inequality or structural racism.

Our business is not to provide fuel to the right over minor disagreements but to continue as artists who are brave, bold and push the boundaries of what can be said and thought.

21/05/2023

Miss S has suddenly swung into my room. She has moved back into her apartment in Rome, which has been adjusted for her to live in. She returns to use the pool: and here she is, next to my bed, smiling, laughing and bursting with news from the outside.

Apparently, there are people out there who are noisy and energetic. There are smells, tastes and activity, and a mad, compelling world that has little to do with illness. It was great to see someone who has successfully made the transition from hospital to home. I was wild with pleasure and some envy that she is able to go about with such freedom and joy.

Isabella and Tracey, who is in London, are working hard to get me out of this place, but it's proving to be a slow, bureaucratic business. When I will return home like Miss S is an open question. But as she points out, she was in a far worse state than I was when she first arrived in this hospital. I should not despair or give up hope, yet. Later that day, I saw her in the gym walking on a frame and I was so pleased for her.

The days here are long. They are filled with a novel thing for me: conversation. Since I lie alone in bed until midday, and my only visitor is Lady G, who has time and much liking for me, she and I must get creative with our discussions. There is no rush, and we have no shared past. Everything I learn is new, and she puts up no barriers to our exploration. We talk about cross-dressing, marrying the wrong person, a friend who was struck by lightning, violent disputes with siblings, and why many people, particularly on the radio, begin their sentences with the word 'so'.

At midday Isabella arrives to take care of me until supper, and we talk until she leaves. A friend asks what we have to say after so long together in this enervating institution, and at first I couldn't think of a reply. 'Everything' would have to be my answer. Again, as with Lady G, our talk rarely ceases, and I never find either of us dull.

Friends continue to visit from London,

bringing gossip about our gang, as well as disquieting talk about the collapse of civilization. My days here are quite different to the way I used to live, where mostly I was reading, writing and shuffling aimlessly around the house, lost in my own head. The only people I saw outside of Isabella were the kids, whom I would walk the dog with in the afternoons.

Since my accident, my life has changed, and I'm in dialogue with people most of the day. I miss my previous existence because of my ability to do certain things, like scratch my arse and go to a restaurant, but these new conversations have proven to be a fascinating innovation.

What are they about, these talks? A serious conversation with a friend about his difficult autistic child. A long discussion about the respective bald heads of Pep Guardiola and Erik ten Hag: whether they shave them daily, and if they worry about their odd, if not peculiar, shape. A discussion with a friend whose son converted to Islam to please the parents of a woman he wanted to live with. Conversations with my sons about the necessity of a new striker at Manchester United and the hideous prices of front men these days. Much talk, as well, about our dog Cairo's recent visit to a pub, the people who tickled and stroked him, and how he loves going on the Tube, where he sits up on the seat. People love telling stories about their dogs, and indeed their entire lives, if you give them the opportunity.

One of my greatest treats as a kid was to be taken to London by my dad at the weekend to watch cricket on TV with my uncles, who lived in Pakistan but spent their summers in Britain. They would drink beer, smoke and invite friends over, devoting the weekend to what they called 'shooting the breeze'. They were a close-knit gang, educated, often cruel, and sometimes bullying. I could see why my father had escaped to the London suburbs, partly to get away from them. He was one of the younger ones, and I saw that he struggled to survive. They would argue over politics, tell jokes and competitively try to amuse one another. It was a great game but dangerous to be around. I loved every minute of being a kid with these men – who I wanted to be like when I grew up.

Conversation is useless in the best sense. It's anti-capitalist – you don't make money out of it; there is no material gain. There is only the pleasure of sitting with another human being, of listening to them, of an ephemeral exchange which has no meaning beyond a shared temporary gratification. There are laughs, jokes, teasings, and serious questions. It is better, less trouble, more fulfilling and longer-lasting than sex.

Conversation is like play for adults; in fact, it *is* play. Serious and unserious, pointless and momentous, conversation is not a meeting, a job or a career. And there is no doubt that some people are better at it than others. You could say that this ability is the most important human characteristic, that the thing we most enjoy about others is their conversation. If they are shit at talking, they are no good to us. Conversely, if people are fascinating, we can't wait to hear what they think.

As significant as talking is the ability to

listen, to want to know others, to enjoy them. You can get better at it, you can develop the skill of listening to what others have to say.

I love secrets – though not so much my own – and one of my favourite parts of conversation is to hear the confidences of others. Secrets are the currency of intimacy. I want to be told things that few others have heard. To do this, you have to cajole, charm, and use silence; you have to be bold and careful, particularly if you don't know the other person so well. But if you are shrewd, you can hear startling and lurid things. Everyone has something to hide, something undisclosed they want you to know, and will tell you given the opportunity. They want to be seen. You could call this 'the novelist's moment', when you hear some horrifically juicy revelation from someone you otherwise consider relatively ordinary. There is no *ordinary*. That's what you realize, if you listen long enough, and wait.

10/06/2023

Things are looking up. We are leaving here on Tuesday and returning to London at last. Strangely, you get attached to places, even when you have spent aeons lying on your back, watching a fly crawl across the ceiling. Each time I returned to bed I looked out for that fly, wondering how it was doing. Had I become that insect, making my way around the same space, looking for a way out? But I knew there was no way out for the fly and one day it was gone.

Isabella has been interred here with me, scratching the back of my neck, shaving me, filing my toenails, reading to me, feeding me, and listening to my complaints. This situation is coming to an end and another situation – perhaps an even more uncomfortable one; we just don't know, we will find out – will be replacing it.

I will be taken in a taxi to the airport, and flown home on a commercial aeroplane, going first to a hospital in West London, and then on to another, followed, I hope, by a longer stay at the specialist rehab facility. Nothing happens for months, then everything happens at once.

This move has been made possible by the efforts of Tracey, and by those of Isabella and Lady G here, as well as by the doctors at Santa Lucia, who have been exceedingly helpful.

I'm looking forward to seeing my city again; in fact I am looking forward to seeing anything at all again. For six months I have looked at nothing but this room and the terrace outside the bar area. The weather is getting warmer, the sun has come out, and soon it will be hot. Time has almost slowed down to a standstill, as it does when you are a child. Not that I led an interesting life before my accident, it's just that I was free.

On another note, years ago I read half a book by Cormac McCarthy but had to put it down. I don't read a lot of fiction. I watch movies, but I don't much like reading or writing made-up stories any more. I don't know why. I read a lot of newspapers, including the shitty ones, and I admire and respect journalists, particularly sportswriters, who I read avidly. It must be difficult for journalists, all that sticking to the truth and trying to make it interesting; all that chasing after facts, looking things up. As for the Cormac McCarthy, the title of which I forget, it was so good I could hardly bear it; some books are like that. My writing started to come out like him, so I had to put the book down and I never went back to it. I wonder whether this is the same for other writers.

Tomorrow, Lady G is taking us out for lunch in central Rome, having been granted special permission by the hospital. This will be a rehearsal for our trip back to London. I can't wait to eat spaghetti alle vongole and have a glass of wine, my first in six months.

17/06/2023

CHELSEA AND WESTMINSTER
HOSPITAL, LONDON

I am back home, or at least, back in my home city. My actual home, the place where I spent most of my time before my accident, is still someway off.

The journey.

It was my first time travelling as a disabled person. Sitting in my wheelchair in the car park outside the hospital in Rome, with Carlo, Kier, Isabella and Lady G accompanying me, my heart sank. I saw they had sent what looked like a builder's van to pick me up and drive me to the airport. It was rackety, old and, more seriously, a bit small. The driver pulled down a shaky ramp, got behind me, and tried to shove me inside. No one has ever described me as tall, but it was clear I would not fit. My head would not go under the roof of the van.

The previous day, I wondered why Isabella had insisted on measuring me twice, perhaps it was for my coffin. Now, Lady G and Isabella discussed removing the cushion under my backside to reduce my height, but pulling it out while I was sitting on it was impossible. There was no way that I could fit into the van without serious damage to the vehicle or to my head.

At last, a larger van was sent for and we made it to the airport. If you are disabled, they put you on the plane first, which is, as you can imagine, a hell in itself. We were delayed for nearly two hours before take-off and then spent another hour stuck on the tarmac in London.

I had to wait for the entire plane to disembark, and as I was sitting at the front on an aisle seat, many of the passengers shoved me as they passed, looking down at me pityingly. Then, I was taken off on the other side of the aircraft on a sort of motorized swizzle stick.

Four hours later, we were in a taxi going over Hammersmith Flyover. I could almost see my house. It was heartbreaking; I wanted to go home and not to another hospital. But I had no choice. I could have wept.

At the new hospital we were kept in A&E until late in the evening; patients were waiting despairingly, and others, clearly drunk or mad, were running up and down the corridors pursued by security.

Now, I am lying in a side room of this hospital. It is a relatively new building but already looks dated, a bit like a 1990s shopping centre. The nurses are cheerful and as sweet as they were in Italy. But in Italy everyone was white. Here, the only white faces I see are those of Isabella and my friends. The accents are multifarious. Several of the doctors and nurses are Indians who have recently come to the UK after Brexit to help prop up the NHS. There are also Africans, Afro-Caribbeans, Thais, Filipinos, Irish, Poles, and so on. The only person here who speaks standard, middle-class English is me. A tone of voice I taught myself in my early twenties, having grown up half-cockney in the South London suburbs, which was full of East Enders who left their neighbourhoods after being bombed in the Blitz.

This side room is in a dementia ward; I need to be isolated, having caught a hospital bug in Italy which is resistant to antibiotics. Family can visit but I've been told I cannot leave the ward or even my room because, apparently, I am a danger to other patients.

The dementia patients are noisy at night and tend to cry out in distress; several of them try to abscond in their pyjamas and have to be restrained.

My spirits are low. I haven't been as depressed as this for a long time. My health is not improving, I am getting worse. Since I haven't received any physiotherapy, my hands feel more rigid than before and my legs feel immovable.

There is a rotation of friends — several writers, a film director, an actor, a TV chef — who visit throughout the day and early evening, keeping me occupied. I'm afraid of being alone and of wearing out the goodwill of others.

I've been told I can leave the hospital for walks if I wear a mask. So, we go out into the street, Isabella pushing me in an unstable wheelchair with no footplates and in which I'm constantly falling forward. Isabella is terrified that she will tip me into the traffic.

She's even more terrified when she hears that I am planning on making a breakout tomorrow. After breakfast, I will be hoisted into this chair and will leave the ward, getting a taxi and heading home, back to the place I left six months ago for the Christmas holidays. Isabella looks justifiably nervous at this mad scheme, but I have got it in my head and will not let it go.

After a terrible night of insomnia, paranoia and anxiety, I decided to abandon the plan to visit my house. It will be too difficult and distressing for both of us. I call out to my friends, and they gather around, listening to my horrendous tale of sleeplessness and fear. I also have cold sweats; I've eaten almost nothing since I arrived here. I feel nauseous most of the time. I can't get over this loss of my former life. I need my friends more than ever and I don't want them to desert me.

27/06/2023

We try to maintain a turnover of visitors, from ten in the morning to nine at night, so that there is always somebody with me. Isabella is here all day, but any visitor is welcome, since they provide distraction from my feeling of being trapped.

The ideal hospital visitor stays for at least one hour. My favourites are the self-absorbed ones, people who talk about themselves, bringing in the outside world. Since I can no longer bear to read the newspapers, watch television or listen to podcasts, other people are my only entertainment. Sometimes guests do voices and imitations – anything to stop me thinking about all that I have lost and whether I will get any of it back.

Some people come only once, to have a look at me and pay their respects. Others come every day; they are my favourites. There are those who stay too long, and those who disappear too quickly to have their hair done. When they leave it's upsetting, since I don't know when I will see them again, and I fear there being a gap between visitors.

One friend who is deafer than he likes to admit sits with his head in his hands, in more or less complete silence, making me feel as morose as he is. Another guest is more miserable than I am, and I feel compelled to try to cheer him up. My boys come most days but usually only for a short time, and one of them is angry that I am ill. But I love hearing about their adventures. Sometimes I am so sullen that I can barely speak.

I have been here longer than I thought. The bureaucracy is maddening. The NHS doesn't like to say yes to any of my demands, refusing to let me go home for the day, or move me to another, less shouty ward. Some of the doctors enjoy bringing bad news, particularly regarding my hospital bug. When they touch me, the nurses wear full PPE garb. It is as if I am a toxic object, even though I am not contagious. A doctor has confirmed that I probably caught this bug in Rome, and that seventy-five per cent of all nurses have it, although they are not tested.

There are rules and protocols that have to be followed. A chirpy psychologist came to see me and I soon reduced her to helplessness. After all, my depressed condition is caused by my reality and not by anything imaginary or historical. After a time, trying to be obliging, she suggested I hire a personal assistant. She also said that when I get home I should get a dog, which might be able to pick things up for me with its teeth, like my phone or my wallet. I informed her that I already have a dog, and he tends to shred things rather than fetch them. Psychologists and psychiatrists in hospitals are, overall, hopeless. There is little they can say, and their only response to most situations is to offer antidepressants.

I am constantly nauseous, which I suspect is caused by constipation. The nurses are always asking whether I have opened my bowels. I am considering writing a hospital story called 'Have You Opened Your Bowels?' I'm sure it would be a hit. I can only open my bowels with the help of an enema, which I have twice a week, and I can only pee with the help of a catheter. Soon I will have a hole drilled into my pubic bone so that I can pee directly into a bag without urinating through my penis.

The constant nausea means I eat little. Maybe half a slice of toast, a cup of tea, some chocolate, a piece of melon and a few mouthfuls of macaroni cheese. Friends try to entice me with delicious dishes but there is nothing so delicious that I want to eat it. All food tastes the same: cardboardy and difficult to swallow. It stays in my mouth for too long. I have no appetite. No libido. My battery is flat.

Once a day I go to the 'gym', a small, grim room off the main thoroughfare of the ward. It is ill-equipped and dark compared to the gyms in the Santa Lucia. This is the NHS. But the physiotherapists are good-natured and enthusiastic. They try to get me moving. They stand me up without the aid of a hoist or a machine, using their hands and bodies instead. The highlight is seeing the Fulham and Chelsea skyline from the window. To my right, I notice a cupboard with a sign on it saying 'Circus Chair Parts and Crutches'.

The nights are the worst. I tend to fall asleep between nine and ten o'clock and wake up around four, with terrible thoughts and loneliness. I am finding it impossible to turn off my mind at that time. If I am lucky I can sleep through until seven. I endure the morning alone until Isabella arrives at midday. When she leaves in the evening, she calls David of Bromley in Canada for me, and he and I talk for an hour and a half. He has a low, sonorous voice and tells entertaining stories which get me in the mood for the night. We call him the Bromley Scheherazade.

I've woken up again. It is 2 a.m. A patient is wailing, another is banging on his table with a spoon. From where I am lying, I can see a disabled, half-naked man dragging himself across the floor pulling a leaking piss bag behind him. Then, a zombie-like patient who regularly approaches my door, now comes in, stands beside my bed and stares at me vacantly, before shuffling off. In the morning, the nurses shut my door and draw the curtains around all the patients' beds. This is how we know they are removing the body of someone who has died during the night.

I need to get out. But I must get my house readjusted before I can think about going home. I wasn't as depressed in Rome because I was looking forward to returning to London. Now I'm in London, it has become a strain and a disappointment, and I feel I am living in an unreal world.

02/07/2023

I have lost my appetite. I cannot eat more than two or three mouthfuls of melon, or of pain aux raisins. Sometimes I have a few cubes of chocolate or a protein drink, and all day a little bit of water.

My biliousness makes me vomit. When I see my sons tucking into massive salmon and cream cheese sandwiches, I am shocked by how much they manage to consume. All food repulses me; there is not a particular taste I am looking for. I have become disillusioned with all my former appetites.

A few weeks ago, David of Bromley began writing long letters about life in Beckenham in the 1970s, his sightings of David Bowie in local coffee shops, and how one summer he took off to Italy on a motorbike, at the behest of a gay leather queen whom he met in a Penge repair shop, and who invited David to live and work in Perugia, in a semi-derelict castle. When, in Italy, the man realized that David was not going to fuck him, he passed him on to an older woman, who had form with younger men.

People say that writing and other forms of artistic expression are cathartic, but David is finding it disturbing and disorientating to think about what these important events in his early life mean to him now. Every day he sends me a new section, Isabella reads it to me, and when she has left the hospital, I ring him to discuss it at length. He's planning on turning these letters into a longer narrative.

Our conversations have helped him to reframe that which he thought he had already absorbed, enabling him to develop his self-understanding. It has been a pleasure for me to get back to teaching. So, this is a good example, and a practical one at that, of someone using art to view their experience from another perspective. He wouldn't have been able to do this alone. It is the presence of at least one other person that has made this possible. These conversations always cheer me up before the long fear and desolation of the night. I have helped him, as I have been helped.

It isn't surprising, since I am depressed and ill, that my libido has died. I discovered in Rome that the doctors were prescribing me a small amount of antidepressants, which I didn't ask for or want. In this new hospital, they have doubled the dose, since I didn't much notice I was taking them anyway. Asking around my friends, it turns out that at least fifty per cent of them have been, or are currently, on antidepressants. Some have been running major institutions on them. One friend, who has reproachful thoughts after midnight, has been taking them for twenty years, and has no intention of giving them up. People ask what particular variety I am taking, but I can never remember the name or pronounce it. I was always opposed to them since I have my own cure in psychoanalysis, which I continue to do once a week, on the phone. One friend said, 'Antidepressants get you to the party and psychoanalysis helps you enjoy it once you get there.' I avoided antidepressants because I didn't want to mess with my brain, which I require for work. But I am beyond that now. I am suffering more than I deserve.

I cannot believe that I have been living on a dementia ward for three weeks. It is worse than a bad joke. The cries and howls are disturbing. Previously I led a lucky life; I had all the luck in the world. Now it has run down.

I have given up fiction for conversation. I can no longer make things up for a living; it seems too artificial in the face of this absurdity. In circumstances like this you really find out who your friends are. I wish I had been kinder; and if I get another chance, I will be.

It is summer, and I am sitting outside the hospital in the ferocious heat, sharing a vape with Sachin. The scene on the street, on this busy road, resembles a slice of Dante's Inferno; the hospital sick, in their wheelchairs, some on drips, many on sticks, dressed in ward gowns, a lot of them smoking, some of them drinking, all in a bad way.

After this I am taken for my walk. Sachin, who is strong, pushes me across the Fulham Road, and we take a bumpy ride down into the heart of South Kensington. He likes to eat in restaurants around here, and I tell him I remember these streets from my drinking days in the 1970s, when the area was rougher and more bohemian. We see nannies pushing prams, Filipino staff walking dogs, and gardeners and builders shifting equipment. As we walk, we comment on the grandeur of the properties around us, most of which appear vacant, and are probably owned by foreign billionaires.

I am having numerous petty disputes with the head nurse about whether I can or cannot have the door to my room left open. I have claustrophobia, panic attacks and hate to feel trapped. The nurse claims that I must keep the door closed. It's difficult for me to argue since I am nauseous and weak, surviving on bits of fruit and yogurt. The doctors have failed to solve this issue, which could be due to the mixture of meds I am on. I try to force myself to eat but it is difficult since food tastes vile. There is discharge from my wound where I had my catheter operation and there may be an infection. I am waiting to find out. The only good news is that in the next few days, I may be moved to a better neurological facility, at Charing Cross Hospital, which is nearby and closer to my house and family.

Sachin insists I should note that interesting people have come to visit me. In my room, which has turned into a talking shop, friends have stimulating discussions about politics, food, sexuality, hospitals and various other subjects. But I struggle to engage. Sachin thinks I will look back on this as a fascinating time, that perhaps meaning can only be found in suffering later on, but at the moment it doesn't feel like that.

19/07/2023

CHARING CROSS HOSPITAL,
LONDON

I left the previous hospital a few days ago, which was a relief. It was a madhouse, noisy and tragic. I was taken in an ambulance to a hospital fifteen minutes down the road, to a neurological ward, where their speciality is patients with spinal injuries.

My new room is small, grey and grim. There is a TV on the wall opposite which doesn't work, despite Sachin's efforts. The view to my left is better; I am high up in the building and can see the sky. Every two minutes a plane passes, crossing the window on its way to Heathrow. I think of the passengers packing up their things and getting ready to disembark, wondering if I'll go on an aeroplane again.

I'm weak and in low spirits, and still trying to eat despite my nausea. The doctor ordered an abdominal X-ray, which demonstrated that I'm full of shit and heavily constipated. A clinical nurse stuck his finger up my arse to try to dislodge some of it, which gave me a tremendous pain, lasting all night and preventing me from sleeping. People pay good money to be fingered. Two of my visitors made the same joke.

I still speak to my analyst on the phone. After thirty years of dreams and silences, we've become more intimate. I tell him how much I love him, and wonder if he'll come here to visit. He tells me to eat despite my disgust, and seems to believe that I can find some living force within myself, that I will not want to give up, as I often feel like doing.

I had a visitor here yesterday, a good friend, and we were gossiping away happily when a more-or-less stranger walked in. I recognized her but had no idea what her name was. Luckily she introduced herself. She's a woman I would see in the supermarket and on Brook Green, where I walk the dog. She found out from a film-producer friend of mine where I was, went to the previous hospital and was redirected here. We talked about films and politics and not long after that she left for a Pilates class. It was strange to be visited by someone I hardly know in such intimate surroundings, in my pyjamas, barely able to speak. The friend who was here was annoyed on my behalf and said she should have called or texted but I don't think she has my number. I wondered whether she was being sympathetic or just inquisitive. She didn't ask me much about myself. I found myself thinking: I'm not a show.

It is quiet here, and at night dead silent. When it gets dark I listen to Radio 4 and take sleeping pills. I try not to think about my misfortunes, even as they mount up. There is more going wrong with my body: at each examination they find some new problem, which makes me worry. Will I ever get out of this, will I die here? I think about killing myself by overdosing. It would be a relief. The other night, I said to David of Bromley it is as if I have been picked on and bullied; someone has made a mistake and got the wrong person; surely they will recognize this injustice and end this farce so I can return to my normal life. But I do realize that this is not a mistake; it is reality, this has happened to me.

I have gone through the door and can never

return. This is my fate. But at least I'm alive, even though I'm stuck in this small grey room, terrified of being left alone. Frightened. Injured.

23/07/2023

Sachin wheels me out of the hospital into the scorching heat. I ask him to pull down my baseball cap and shield my eyes. To the left there is a gloomy car park; in front a squalid walkway between two filthy ponds. You can see from here that the hospital is crumbling: there are wires and panels hanging down, and the place is in serious need of reconstruction. Inside, the lifts are chaotic and sometimes don't work. Outside, the revolving doors are often stuck. The council cannot decide whether to knock the hospital down or refit it. Since the junior doctors are also on strike, it is difficult not to see all this as another symbol of British decline.

I am being pushed down the Fulham Palace Road, which is clogged with traffic. In my wheelchair, I feel frail and vulnerable. People are literally looking down on me. I cannot believe that they don't know what it is to wake up every morning and find you cannot use your hands — what an ending it is.

I'm pushed into the barber shop where a friendly Syrian gives me a shave and a haircut. I'm shocked by my appearance; I look thin, if not emaciated. My eyes and nose are bigger than before. But I have been successfully shitting after taking a barrage of laxatives and my appetite has returned. I had a halloumi sandwich for lunch, which is more than I've eaten since I've come back from Italy. I feel warmer.

This place is certainly an improvement. It's quieter. There are no half-naked demented people crawling along the floor, although this hospital is not without its nutters. There is one guy with a bad injury who, despite being barely able to walk, managed to smash up his room last night while abusing the nurses, and had to be restrained by security. I am tired for most of the day, go to sleep early, afraid of my dreams; I wake up around eleven at night and, in my restlessness, listen to Martin Amis's superb *Money* as an audiobook. It is as funny and outrageous as I remember. But last night, around midnight, two young African nurses were changing me

while I was listening to *Money* on my Alexa. I
had reached the place in the book where John
Self, the protagonist, decides to try to rape his
girlfriend. It's a comic and nasty scene which
hasn't aged well, but which reminds us of how
transgressive literature can be. The nurses were
horrified as the language became more fruity; I
was embarrassed and had to turn it off. So much
for literature.

My friends still visit most days; some of
them come early, others late, and some just
walk in at random times. Occasionally there are
four visitors in this squalid little room at once,
people who in other circumstances wouldn't
meet. Carlo says my life is not so banal, since he
considers my friends to be interesting: writers,
intellectuals, artists, journalists, directors, TV
people, and so on. The liberal elite are in and
out, crossing over with one another, leaning
against the wall, trying to find a chair, sitting
on the edge of the bed, eating chocolate and,
in the evening, poppadoms, discussing books,
holidays, their children, and the failure of the
Tory government. Apparently, I've got quite

a party going on here, but since I refuse to be cheered up, I can only vaguely enjoy it.

I prefer it if Carlo is here when other people come, since he can do the heavy lifting in the conversation. He has plenty to say, he likes to talk. Until today, when I started to eat again, I've been too weak to say much. It costs me a lot to speak. Now I can feel some of my strength returning. But the stronger I am, the more clearly I comprehend the reality of my situation.

Holidays are the topic I hate most, since people say things like 'I'm away now, off to Tuscany for two weeks, but I'll see you when I get back.' Two weeks! They assume I'll still be sitting in this shitty room in my nappy in two weeks' time and they will be right. Think how many nights I will have to get through. I'm going nowhere. No wonder I feel like shit. Fuck them, their holidays and their fucking happiness.

Late at night, around ten thirty, the nurses come in, turn the big lights on and give me my medication. If I've had a shit, they clean me up and change me. I'm handled and turned and washed by strangers every night. It is no longer humiliating. I have no dignity left. What bothers me is being among strangers; the nurses know one another and often chat as they work. They are kind and professional, but they swap around a lot and I can't get to know them.

It is unusual to me, someone who has spent their life doing exactly what they want, to now be in this straitjacket, to have lost my agency and independence.

What I want is to start going home, even for a few hours, since I live only fifteen minutes from this hospital. I could do a sort of day-release. I haven't seen my house since the Christmas holidays.

29/07/2023

An old friend came in with an envelope of photographs. He pulled one out; it was of me, taken in Cork in 1993. I am at a book signing, handing to someone a paperback copy of *The Buddha of Suburbia*. I am wearing a Levi's jacket and a Paul Smith scarf, which I still have. My hair is long and black and tucked behind my ears. The light is on my face, which is smooth and pixie-like. I am in my late thirties.

Without asking, the friend pins the photograph to the wall opposite my bed. I am not sure I want it, but there it is, and I am looking at it now. People come in and say, in amazement, 'Is that you?' Now I am gaunt and unshaven with straggly hair, and, like all of us, barely resemble the person I once was. The picture reminds me of all that I have lost.

I am mainly in bed at the moment rather than my wheelchair, due to a fissure in my arse, which the clinical nurse identified after looking up there with a torch and a camera. I am taking liquid morphine to alleviate the pain and trying to find a position that is less sore. When you're in pain, it is all you can think about. The whole thing is depressing as hell. I stare at this picture and realize there is no going back. The kids come in and say that what I am going through, all my suffering, is temporary. That is a useful reminder.

This morning, in the unit's kitchen, I took part in a physical therapy group with four other patients. Since I am in a single side room, I rarely see anyone else. We gathered around the table, playing with blocks and kids' toys. One of the women was young, around thirty, and was beautiful, resembling Jackie Kennedy. She could barely speak or use her hands. The four physiotherapists were all upbeat, exaggeratedly so, talking to us slowly, with a forced brightness, as if they were presenting a children's programme. In contrast, the patients looked dazed, as if they couldn't believe their misfortune. Their sadness was palpable. I was glad to be with them, though none of us spoke to one another. Jackie Kennedy inexplicably started to weep and had to be rushed out.

Sachin comes in and I reproach him for being late. My family and close friends are on a relay system so that I am never alone during the day. But sometimes there are gaps, which I do not enjoy, since I have dreadful thoughts when I'm alone. As Sachin feeds me, he says, 'I hope we're not going to have to do this for the rest of your life.' I look at my withered hands, which are not improving much, and say, 'I think you are.'

Carlo assures me that I am making improvements; my legs are stronger and the physiotherapist has advised us that my arms will come back later, when I have gained strength in my core and shoulders. He says I have every right to be gloomy, but the doctors and physios are more optimistic than I am.

When Carlo and Sachin set out to become screenwriters, the three of us, in various combinations, would walk around West London every afternoon talking about stories, structure, and how to succeed in the industry. We would start with an idea or image, and then string it out, develop it, until it began to look like a whole narrative. It was fun and satisfying; we enjoyed being together. We still do.

I never wanted to be just a screenwriter. What I liked was the freedom to work in several forms. When I got stuck on a movie, I would write a short story, then I would work on an essay or a novella. To be a screenwriter is to be entirely dependent on the industry, on others. When I wrote films, they were usually for particular directors: Stephen Frears, Udayan Prasad – who made *My Son the Fanatic*, a film I am proud of – and my friend Roger Michell. I could write these films on spec, knowing they would almost certainly get made. It wouldn't turn out to be wasted time, as so much screenwriting is these days.

I was fortunate to be able to make a living my whole life, but at times it was a bit touch and go. There were periods in the 1980s when it was possible to earn significant money from writing novels, and I was able to buy a house. I'm not sure my kids will have the same security, and I worry about them. A lot of my friends' kids have gone into the same profession as their parents. I was glad my sons had found something they wanted to do with their lives, something meaningful, which gave them a sense of direction and purpose. Lying in this hospital bed, day in and day out, is like being in a bad job, wasting time, waiting for time to pass.

05/08/2023

A right-wing acquaintance comes to visit me, someone I met just once before, during lockdown. We liked each other and became friends immediately; I like his conversation, which is always amusing or informative. He says that the problem with Rishi Sunak is that his voice is too high. He's not convincing as a leader. I say I can imagine Sunak in a white coat, behind the counter of a pharmacy discussing haemorrhoid creams. My friend says the politicians with deeper voices do much better. It is unfortunate for people of the left that Keir Starmer sounds robotic and mindless, as if he were reading from a menu. My visitor says that men with deep voices make for the best seducers. He adds that David Beckham's voice undermines his masculinity, which is still considerable. As I try to fall asleep later, waking up approximately every twenty minutes, wondering if the clock has stopped, I consider all of this. The actor Brian Blessed, known for his booming voice, must be quids in, a master of the universe.

My family and I have been planning a brief trip home this weekend. But the clinical nurse is adamant that a physiotherapist should visit my home first, to ensure, as he puts it, that the place is 'safe' for me and my wheelchair. I wonder if this guy has the right to tell me where I can and can't go; I haven't been kidnapped, I am not a prisoner.

And so, the following morning I'm in my wheelchair and Isabella pushes me out of the hospital and across the Fulham Palace Road to the bus stop. Almost straight away a bus comes, its ramp slides out and I'm shoved on. Ten minutes later, I am on the Shepherd's Bush Road where Tracey and Cairo meet me. This is the first time I've seen Cairo, our golden retriever, since my accident, and I wonder if he recognizes me; after all, he loves everyone.

Together we walk down the familiar street towards my house. It has been eight months since I've been here. I don't want to become upset, and I try to imagine I've been away on a long holiday. Isabella and Tracey push me inside and Carlo joins us. Thankfully the place is the same, except that I am at a lower angle; I can't get an overview as I could before. The chair is uncomfortable, and I know I won't be able to stay long before I have to go back to bed in the hospital. I am glad Isabella has been living here since we returned to London, although she has allowed the garden to become overgrown. In another life I would be out there with a machete, but she loves it this way, where she entertains foxes, birds and squirrels.

We have lunch and sit together with the dog. I wish I could go upstairs and see my study again, and the bedroom, but that is impossible. I sit in my chair at the bottom of the stairs looking up, but it is maddening, there is no way I can get to my study. I imagine my two desks, one facing the wall and the other the window overlooking the street; I think of my psychoanalytic library, my collection of creative writing books, and my scores of pens, and wonder whether I should give them to my sons, since I won't be using them. Isabella says it's too soon to do that; we mustn't give up.

We discuss what adjustments will need to

be made to the house for it to become habitable again.

On Sunday, Isabella and Kier push me to the Thames, near Hammersmith Bridge, and we walk along the riverside path, up to the River Cafe. I've lived in this area, around West Kensington and Barons Court, since I was a student in 1976 and have cycled this way scores of times. Kier says he remembers being a kid and taking long rides with me, and, not so long ago, Isabella and I used to walk Cairo along the river path. The dog was more of a menace then, and loved to take a dive into the Thames. It was always a lot of trouble to persuade him to come out, covered in thick mud. One time, while barrelling across Ravenscourt Park, he tore a woman's hijab from her head and ran off with it in his teeth; another time he stole a blind man's cane. He still steals the balls of other dogs and can cause mayhem during picnic season.

I've started to have long, lurid and convoluted dreams. They are like novellas. A friend suggests this may be a side effect of the antidepressants.

The other night I woke up in a cold sweat yelling my head off, dreaming I was being swallowed by a snake. A nurse rushed into my room, worried I was losing my mind, asking: Where was I? What was my name? Who was the Prime Minister? I had to think.

My analyst will be pleased with the dreaming, but not with antidepressants, which he is against, since they muffle feeling, and render you less able to marshal your resources. A psychiatrist, visiting me here, said rather sarcastically, 'Psychoanalysts understand nothing about drugs.' I'm sure there are many psychoanalysts who would say that psychiatrists know little about minds.

At present I am engaged in a minor struggle with a night nurse who is very officious. He's fond of the rules and he has told me that he must wake me up at six in the morning to wash and dress me. I've told him several times that I should be washed and dressed at nine according to my schedule, which is on the wall, but he chooses to ignore this and refuses to look at it. He glances at my medical schedule – which is on the mobile computer, a cumbersome machine he drags around with him – and tells me he needs to digitally evacuate my arse, to ease my constipation. He waves his finger about threateningly as an illustration. I tell him that I don't want any of his fingers anywhere near my arse, but he insists this is a medical necessity.

These little battles between nurses and patients, about who has authority over whom, go on all the time. Some nurses hate to be contradicted; after all, they have experience and knowledge. On the other hand, the patient knows their own body and if, like me, you've been in a hospital for months on end, you get to know which nurses know what they are doing. Some lack confidence, and others like you to know who is in charge. If you spend twenty-four hours a day under the care of nurses, you soon figure out their characters. I wonder whether, if I had a deeper voice, I might be taken more seriously in here.

14/08/2023

Sex is never mentioned in hospital. There are no jokes, double entendres, or even exchanged looks. The place is antiseptic in all senses. Of the many losses I have suffered due to this accident and injury, sexual feeling might be the least of it. A friend who had prostate cancer, and can never have sex again, said, 'Thank God I'm alive, and every day I'm glad to be. That's enough.'

Losing one's sexuality overnight, in a sudden blow, is like losing a sense. Something that has guided and activated you throughout your life is unexpectedly missing. To have no erections, to feel no sexual excitement nor have any fantasies, is to be deprived of an orientating engine that has steered, bedevilled and pursued you since adolescence. It is a major absence, and a puzzling one. I now look at sexuality from another point of view, that of a disinterested spectator. I wonder what all the fuss is about. Why people are risking their reputations for the sake of what seems now to be an unimportant, if not minor, excitement? It doesn't follow that I feel no enthusiasm; I do, just not for *that*.

For me, trying to understand sexuality is a bit like attempting to grasp the strange fetishes of others: if someone has a wild passion for hats, donkeys or umbrellas, this may seem inexplicable to the onlooker. Yet we know that many people do have these passions, and that they are incurable, lifelong, and whole societies are often unconsciously structured around them. To be in the thrall of a fetish, addicted to high-heel shoes, for instance; spending your life fantasizing and surrounding yourself with them could be all-consuming and destructive. What an inconvenience and how corrosive it would be to your other relationships. All sexuality feels like this to me now: foreign, almost alien.

Many of my stories, films and novels have been ordered around the bewitching mischief of sexuality; its play and performance, of people desiring other people's bodies. Sexuality is also seemingly irrational compared to other motivating forces like money, vengeance and social aspiration. It is a wonderful excuse for writers to add more than a dash of madness into their subjects. Some people really want sex, but they only want specific kinds of sex and certain kinds of people, and they will give up a lot to get it, sometimes even their lives.

But you can live without it; a lot of people do. And when you think of how little time you actually spend having sex — what a tiny proportion of your life is in fact given over to it, compared to, say, watching television — it is amazing that so many stories are devoted to its mystery and power. Being on the other side now, an observer, I'm still curious and will continue to be; but I've lost something that was once imperative, and more than that, I'm even wondering why it was important, mattering so much to so many.

I sit outside the hospital in my wheelchair looking at the strange creatures in their crazy clothing or hospital gowns, with their tattoos or blue hair, lost limbs and mad aspect, and wonder what sort of sexuality governs them, or if it does at all. There are plenty of people about, hundreds if not thousands of them, getting on and off buses, or cycling furiously up the road. Someone somewhere sometime must be having sex, since the world's population continues to increase, except in Italy.

I have a friend who liked to have sex every day, or at least she did before she had children. We all know people who appear not to have had sex for years; we speculate whether they miss it, and if they masturbate at all – and if so, how often. I have another friend, same age as me, who is attractive and always horny, and whose husband, due to an accident, has become unavailable. It has been a difficult thing, but she has become reconciled to the reality of the situation – she loves and respects him, and will live with it.

Sex, of course, isn't just genital. Who can say where it starts and where it ends? Think of kissing, caressing and enjoying the bodies of others; think of looking and speaking, whispering, and fantasizing – all are forms of sexuality, spread everywhere, and are present all the time. These pleasures will never be denied me, but at the moment they do not have the same point or influence. If once sexual feeling was there strongly, it is now gone; a strange lack, a sort of bafflement about what went on before and what it must have meant.

There are few places less romantic than hospitals, where relationships are mostly functional, and there is little space for enjoyment. At lunchtime most days, Isabella hurries into my room and feeds me. In the evenings, she orders my favourite daal and rice from the Palace Tandoori, where they know her now. When we were in Rome, we would either eat at home, or drive into the historical centre, and dine outside in some romantic spot, walking about the city late at night, the most dreamy place in the world, with inconceivable things to see at every corner.

Isabella has been broken by this accident. She finds it almost impossible to work; her concentration is shot. I feel guilty and responsible for her fatigue, if not exhaustion. But what can I do about it? She lives in my house alone, away from her family and friends. How playful we used to be. Whether we can get back to some form of erotic mischievousness is unanswerable right now. Will we ever find each other mysterious and intriguing again?

23/08/2023

'We're not very good with groups, are we, Hanif?' said the physiotherapist.

We were on our way to a local café: four of us in wheelchairs, two patients walking, and three physiotherapists.

Jackie Kennedy was bent sideways, weeping silently. Another patient was dribbling, and of the two men walking, one could only say a few words in a foreign language, which he repeated constantly, along with what sounded like bird-chirping noises. This is the man who comes into my room late at night. Probably he wants to complain about the noise of my radio, but since he can't speak, he just stares at me. It is frightening.

Now, this strange caravan tumbles towards the river, at Hammersmith, near the Riverside Studios, where I worked at the end of the 1970s and early 80s, a place that I considered to be my real university, and where I learned about theatre, dance and literature, spending time with writers, directors, actors and producers.

One of the physiotherapists says to me, 'Have we been here before, Hanif?' I didn't know what to say or where to begin. I feel melancholic being by the river again, on this spot where I had spent some of my young life, enjoying this view and trying to become an artist.

A year ago, I couldn't begin to conceive what a hell my life would become. So it wouldn't be unnatural for me to wonder, as I sit by the river, what the fuck I am doing here, and whether I will ever escape this present hell. This gaggle of people are sad to be among, and I am one of them now, falling forward in my chair, with my head drooping on my shoulders, feeling too heavy to hold up. Is this really me? Is this reality? But it is. I am living in the hospital, and there is no prospect of me going home anytime soon. I am waiting in a kind of limbo before I can be moved to the new rehab.

Carlo sits here on the eighth floor, wearing a baseball cap, T-shirt, shorts and trainers. He is so beautiful, brown and young. I lean forward in my wheelchair dictating these notes to him, watching the planes cross the sky, and becoming increasingly impatient and short-tempered.

The gym in this place is nothing like as well equipped as the ones in Rome. On each floor of the Santa Lucia, there was an excellent gym, with a good complement of physios. Here, the gym is crowded, with physios working at their computers at one end, and patients at the other. The machines and equipment are old-fashioned, inadequate and sometimes broken, despite this being a neurological ward. The physios seem to leave and be replaced constantly, and few of them appear to have the skill and knowledge of their Roman counterparts. Which isn't to say there are not exercises I can do most days, which are necessary to keep me functioning. I am given only an hour of physio a day by the hospital, and so in the early evening I work with a private physio who comes in to exercise me in my bed, which stops me deteriorating. I am exercised in my hands, legs and stomach, and I also do movements in my wheelchair with Kier.

I know these are good for me, though I complain, but I am not sure whether I am in fact improving, or just remaining the same. There is not much I can do for myself at the moment; I still cannot hold a pen, type, stand or open a book. Apparently, progress is incremental; I have to work on myself every day. I guess it is a bit like writing.

It is an agony to be me. I want to punish those around me, while knowing that no one can be blamed for this situation. I had an accident, that's all, a random contingent event, with no connection to logical meaning.

02/09/2023

At the opening of one of my favourite plays, Chekhov's *The Seagull*, the character Medvedenko asks the maudlin Masha, 'Why do you always wear black?' She replies, 'I'm in mourning for my life.' As far as I can remember, we never really find out what life exactly she is in mourning for, but it is a line that has resonated with me a lot lately, being in mourning for one's life: it is haunting, like a piece of music.

I once had a full and enjoyable life, and then one day I had an accident, and that life was over. But I didn't quite die; I almost did. As I lay on my head in Rome, on a wooden floor in a pool of blood, with Isabella crouched down beside me, I felt death coming for me – I believed I had just a few breaths left, and I remember feeling enraged that I had to die in this ignoble way, when I was quite keen to carry on living, there were plenty of things I still wanted to do. It was an affront, I wasn't ready, that was what annoyed me. I thought of my dear friend Roger

Michell, who was younger than me and who, not long ago, went to bed and failed to wake up.

I have continued to exist in this crooked form while thinking about how I lived before and wondering whether I could ever get back to some semblance of it. There was literally a break, a rupture, between the two parts of my life. In my mind, I'm still living in the first, while in my body, unfortunately, I am in the second, broken measure.

Recently I had an MRI scan, and it looks like I have had some mini strokes in the past. Many people over fifty have these; they are common, and there may be no symptoms. These mini strokes, as they are called, are not connected to my accident, but for me, they are an extra thing to worry about, since there is a danger I may have another one. The hospital tried to give me a test to ascertain whether my mental facilities are still all there. I glanced through the pages of the test – which were a series of questions, pictures and basic arithmetic – and it was so simple and childish I refused to participate. I haven't yet lost my mind as far as I know, though I am aware that I have less energy and my speech is slower.

One of the things about Chekhov's great plays, particularly *Uncle Vanya* and *The Seagull*, is that they concern friendship; his work is full of people just hanging around together, even if they haven't chosen each other, or don't like one another much.

During lockdown I wrote a play, *The Spank*, which concerns two middle-aged male friends falling out over a relatively minor incident which strains, tests and then ruins the friendship. The play was performed in Italy, toured all over the country and was successful. In the introduction to the published edition, I wrote an essay about friendship in which I discussed how a bond is tested, taken to its limit, and finally broken. Now, in my situation, relationships are tested in new ways.

I have been living in hospital since Boxing Day, which is an unusual situation. When I was a teenager, my father was often ill with heart problems and during those years he spent a lot of time hospitalized. I visited him often, but would sit there reading the newspapers. It was excruciating to see him so brought down, this man whom I admired and considered strong and potent. I wanted to be elsewhere, living the life of a teenager, but felt obliged to be with him, and when I wasn't there I felt guilty. Dad had failed to become the novelist he wanted to be, which had depressed him and brought gloom into our family, and now he was suffering physically. It was a lot for a kid to worry about.

Most people will be in hospital at some point in their lives, but it is uncommon for a patient to live in one as I have been doing, for months on end.

I have learned that a hospital ward is an ecosystem in itself: the nurses, physiotherapists, doctors, patients and visitors are all connected; they come and go; it is a network full of pleasures and conflicts. One day last December, I was moved from the real world into this soap opera, where I have existed ever since. I experience it as a torture and punishment; I feel it as dismemberment. How it exists in my mind is a horror; I have to be reminded by my friends of its reality, and the possibility of some kind of recovery, and even a future.

Yesterday I picked up a small bottle with my left hand, although I couldn't grip it for long. This morning I stood up on a hoist for about fifteen minutes, and even used my knees to squeeze up and support myself. It is amazing how difficult it is to walk if you can't do it. What an incredible amount of muscular activity goes into walking across a pub, for instance, to order a pint of Guinness. I wonder if it is something I will do again. It seems like such an achievement when you are on the other side.

09/09/2023

'Let's have a look at his penis,' said one of the doctors to the other. Both were young and elegant, and obviously clever. 'Is that okay?'

'Sure, go ahead, feel free,' I said. I almost added, 'These are words I've waited a long time to hear.'

The doctor fumbled in the front of my Paul Smith pyjamas, opened them up, and reached into the mass of overgrown, grey pubic hair. At last, she found the mushroom and bent over to take a closer gander.

'No,' she said, after a momentous wait, 'there is no discharge. It's fine.'

What a relief, I thought; at last, one part of my body that isn't either broken or malfunctioning. Still, I had no idea why she thought there might be a discharge from my penis, and I didn't want to ask.

Before my accident, nobody ever touched me; of course, Isabella did from time to time, but otherwise no one. Now, I am turned, rolled, prodded and poked constantly, and when I say constantly, I mean constantly – every day and every night. I have had more strangers touch my body in the past nine months than I have in my entire life. I have become used to it. Instruments in my ears, fingers up my arse, wash pads around my genitals, under my arms and over my back, lights in my eyes. Everything everywhere, all the time. How did I go from being a private man to a public piece of meat? Naturally, as I've said before, the nurses are kind; I am their work and responsibility, and they are proud of the work they do on me. I see it in their faces and hear it in their voices; I am how they express themselves.

It would be even more difficult to live this life if you were shy about being manhandled, if you had too much dignity, or feared being humiliated. I am already humiliated. It began a long time ago. There isn't much further to fall, and I have to collaborate with the nurses, as they push and pull and roll me here and there. After all, they are not ashamed as they insert a suppository, watch me do a shit and say proudly,

'My, that's a big one' or 'Today, it was only a moderate one, maybe tomorrow we'll have more luck.'

I have to continue to be amused about this; there is nothing else for it, I am neither stoical nor brave, I do nothing out of the ordinary, I am a victim of fate.

I need to repeatedly remind myself of something Salman Rushdie told me during the early years of the fatwa: that the one thing he needed to learn was patience.

16/09/2023

Mornings are the worst, if it could be said that there is indeed a *worst* in all this. The whole thing is terrible, though there are some amusements, mostly to do with other people. But it is in the morning, when I wake up and begin to become conscious of myself, a bit like Gregor Samsa at the beginning of Kafka's *Metamorphosis*, that I realize what has happened to me is real.

Waking up, my body, after a night spent in one position, begins to shift. My first movement may well be a shudder, during which my whole frame, briefly, goes into spasm, as if I have received an electric shock. I realize that my hands and feet are not really my own, that they seem to be injured, unfamiliar objects. I can't move them as I expect to; it is like, as we say in common parlance, your body going to sleep.

A year ago, when I would wake up, I'd stick my legs out of the bed, stand up, and walk into the bathroom for my morning pee. During this pee, I would enjoy looking out of the window at my garden, and the gardens and houses across the way. Somehow, I still expect to be doing that, and I cannot come to terms with the fact that I will never do such an everyday thing again. It is a realization that I cannot bear or take in. So, for me, waking up is like re-entering a horror movie that I had thought, for a moment, I could turn off.

I can do nothing for myself. I am entirely dependent on other people, and am waited on for everything I want. You might say this is a wonderful luxury, but I would like to be able, from time to time, to make myself a cup of tea. But now I cannot be afraid to ask others for things, for them to make me a cup of tea, or to scratch the inside of my ear. I was more inhibited before; I wasn't the asking kind, I wanted to believe that others might intuit my wishes. But if I ever thought that making a demand or asking for something might be a nuisance, I can't worry about that now, since I cannot do anything for myself, and all I have left is speech.

I often wonder whether others are tired of

my demands, or whether I am treating them as though they were my servants. The other day Sachin, who often becomes annoyed with me, finding my condition particularly painful and arduous, burst out, 'You are always asking for things, Dad, and you never say please or thank you!'

I was devastated because since speech is my lifeline, I make sure that I ask for things in the nicest possible way; I have to seduce rather than insist. But I must confess that I do sometimes omit to say please or thank you, it is true, as otherwise I would be saying please and thank you all fucking day long.

There is no way round this: all my conversations with friends, family, nurses and doctors are transactional. What do I want them to do for me? What am I asking for this time? These demands do bring out the best in others; they pity me, love me, identify with me — after all, this could be them one day; how would they feel? How would they behave? What would they want?

What would it be like to be me, they must wonder: a turtle, upturned on its back, waving its little arms and legs around helplessly, begging to be turned over. So, I have become a dictator, and a reluctant one at that. I don't do it out of a sense of omnipotence, but out of weakness. If I am in a rage, as I often am, it is out of powerlessness.

The other day, I was with Kier. He left, and there was an interval of about ninety minutes before Carlo joined me. During that time, when there was nothing good on the radio, I was alone in my wheelchair and couldn't move. I could call for a nurse, but I didn't want a nurse nor any abstract connection. I wanted to – and believed I could for a moment – put my feet on the floor, walk out of here, get the bus and stroll home. In a part of myself, I still believe that is possible; it is hard to relinquish what you once took for granted.

It's not even a year since I became this turtle on its back, and I am not used to it. It is something I will never understand; it is part of me, and yet is beyond me.

23/09/2023

Isabella has returned to Rome to see her family and to work, and the boys and Tracey have been looking after me. Tracey puts me to bed most nights, and we have the opportunity to sit and talk, as we haven't been able to in years, renewing our relationship.

I met her in the mid-1980s after *My Beautiful Laundrette* had been released and was successful around the world, before Stephen Frears and I started shooting *Sammy and Rosie Get Laid*. I was living alone in a one-bedroom flat in West Kensington, in the process of splitting up with my former cohabitee and university girlfriend, Sally. Tracey was working as an associate producer on Jonathan Ross's *Last Resort*. She had been brought up in nearby Chiswick, read English at Oxford, and her father had been a TV director and producer. Since the success of *My Beautiful Laundrette*, the resurgence of Channel 4 and the production companies that fed it, along with the growth of the new media through the 1980s, London had once again become a vibrant and interesting place. Tracey had more contacts than I did, and she took me out into the energizing landscape that was developing in and around Soho. The Groucho Club was at the centre, but there were new bars and restaurants opening all the time. Tim Bevan, Salman Rushdie, Daniel Day-Lewis, Stephen Frears and others of our circle were out and about most nights. It was a cultural renaissance analogous to that of the mid-1960s with pop, and the mid-1970s with punk.

On 14 February 1989 – I remember this day, because it was also the date of the fatwa against Rushdie – I left Barons Court Road for a beautiful two-storey flat I had bought nearby on Comeragh Road, overlooking the Queen's Club tennis courts. It was light and spacious, with a balcony, where I would grow marijuana plants and write. Tracey and I lived there together for a couple of years before we split and she moved to Notting Hill. A few months later, we resumed our relationship and she became pregnant with our twins. After leaving television, she

was working at my publishing house, Faber &
Faber, which had been enjoying a revival under
the fiction editor Robert McCrum and chair-
man, Matthew Evans, where the writers included
Seamus Heaney, Harold Pinter, Kazuo Ishiguro
and P. D. James, among others.

I had some money at last and we bought a
house together in Shepherd's Bush, where Tracey
and I lived with the children. After a couple of
years we split up for good and I returned to my
flat in Comeragh Road, and in 1997 bought a
house a couple of streets away, where I still live,
or would if I could leave this hospital.

Kier came in on Monday lunchtime, bringing
me the tuna and cucumber sandwich from Pret
that I like, as well as a flat white from the Por-
tuguese coffee shop in the Hammersmith mall.
He then took me out for a walk by the river,
saying it was probably the last good day of the
year. As always, we discussed his dating scene,
his outings to the gym and the prospects of
our beleaguered, beloved Manchester United.
Then off he went to work, cycling around the

neighbourhood, teaching piano and guitar to young children.

After, Sachin came bouncing in on his white cushioned trainers, and I was pleased to see he was in a good mood. Sitting down next to my bed, we had a long discussion about his work as a writer, how difficult it was to get started, and we tried to compare the beginning of his career with mine. When you are a young writer, you never know for sure if you're going to make it; whether in fact you will become a professional writer or just fade away, as so many others do, inevitably.

Then we talked about my friends' children and what they might or might not do if they were in the same position as my kids. Would they visit a parent in hospital every day, or would they go missing? Does this sense of love and duty apply to everyone? It is not a question someone can answer until it happens to them.

My friendship with the boys has been altered and matured. I never had any reason to rely on them as I have since my accident. My demands on them have been profound, and they have responded commendably, almost without complaint.

In the evening, Tracey returned. Along with Isabella, she was instrumental in getting me back to London. She makes the cheese and onion sandwiches I like, and in the evenings, when Isabella isn't around, she picks up the tarka daal, prawn bhuna, pilau rice and poppadoms from the Palace Tandoori. I like to eat the same things every day, it doesn't bother me, as long as I don't have to eat hospital food.

Tracey and I discuss her work, the dog, the kids, the state of the nation, and the history of the locale where the hospital is located. Tracey informs me that I will be leaving here next Thursday for the long-hoped-for rehab facility. At last.

Still, I am apprehensive about this move since it is in North London, about an hour away from where we all live. But my stay there will not be open-ended. The staff prepare you for independent life in the outside world, to get you as well as they can before you return home.

30/09/2023

Even when awake I find my mind free-associating, thinking over my life as I have never done before. Since I've become disabled, many of my dreams are violent and unpleasant, and most of them are set in my childhood home in Bromley, which is decayed, if not falling down, or a kind of bomb site. There are characters in wheelchairs, but never me, though I assume that these ghostly figures are parts of me, distributed throughout the dream.

I've been interested in dreams since my uncle, one of my father's many brothers – who was a child psychologist, and ran a school for autistic children in Somerset – first began to talk to me about psychoanalysis. In his book-lined Somerset study in a village called Williton, we'd have long discussions about Shakespeare, racism, politics and literature. He was a man who never wanted to stop educating himself. It was during one of our talks that he told me, quite abruptly, that I wanted to kill my father and sleep with my mother. This was a shocking, if not reductive, view of the Oedipus complex. I became fascinated from that moment by Freud and his work.

At King's College London, where I read philosophy, there was a course given by Richard Wollheim on Freud and psychoanalysis, with a particular interest in the work of Melanie Klein, whom I think he knew, or had been analysed by. Wollheim wrote an excellent book for the Fontana Modern Masters series on Freud, which I studied. Then I read all of Wittgenstein's writing on Freud, which is strange and inaccurate but illuminating. Wittgenstein's sister was analysed by Freud, and their families, both living in Vienna, knew one another.

After leaving King's, my interest in psychoanalysis continued, and I read most of the masters: Winnicott, Klein, Lacan, and so on, and later the modern interpreters, like Adam Phillips and Darian Leader. There is much in this tradition that I found fulfilling and fascinating, particularly the case studies from an earlier period. As far as I can tell, analysts no longer write case studies, for all kinds of reasons, mainly to do with privacy and psychoanalytic accuracy, but I found them as beguiling as good short stories. We know that Freud, when he was writing his own important case studies, worried that they were more like short stories than they were scientific work. It is obvious there is really nothing scientific about them. You could take the same patient and have them analysed by five different therapists, and each analyst would come up with a different view of the analysand. This cannot be how science works.

I began my analysis in the early 1990s, when I was in my late thirties, with a Freudian who was not much older than me, though inevitably, in what psychoanalysts call transference, I considered him to be far more knowledgeable, intelligent and omniscient than I could ever be. I knew immediately he was good at his job.

I had a lot to talk about and found that I looked forward to the sessions, which were twice a week. I took to lying down on the couch with enthusiasm. I didn't want to look at him; I wanted to dream and think. There was a lot of silence, which I was not intimidated by. I had no desire to babble. I found the pauses practical and useful, as Freud suggested they might be. In the silence, a lot is happening; you are not paralysed but thinking; a number of ideas and images will emerge, which will be sorted through until you find something that must be exposed to the light.

People worry therapy will somehow halt the creative process; they suggest that when talking through your issues, you will evacuate them, and have nothing to write about. This was never my fear; it didn't happen. At the end of each session, I wrote a diary entry, in which I would go through the dream interpretations provided in the analysis. This was fertile for my work because the analyst – in a good session – would say things that I could never have conceived myself. He would make surprising, generative connections.

This isn't to say that the sessions were all play. During those years, I went through some painful experiences when I was at a loss and depressed. But the analysis kept everything going. When it works, it doesn't allow you to linger in any particular state of mind. It moves things along, despite the darkness. There is no doubt, however, that psychoanalysis is both a quick and a slow cure. Sometimes during a session you might come to realize some idiotic repetition that you've been living in for most of your life. Something like this could become clear to you, and in that moment you would never wish to make the same mistake again. And while it might be a banal thing, it may have taken you years to come to this recognition. A habit might be impossible to give up, even though to others it might seem simple. Which is why, as I say, psychoanalysis can work both slowly and suddenly.

Freud was an orthodox analyst, but he didn't like an analysis to go on for too long. The idea that a therapist would see the same patient for thirty years or so would have seemed absurd to him. He saw patients for around two years, and then he'd encourage them to leave. But he also socialized and went on holiday with them, gave them money, and he particularly liked wealthy Americans. Lacanians have a particular bias against Americans and what they like to think of as American forms of therapy; but this is a prejudice and an absurd one at that. They like to claim that American therapy shaped patients into becoming part of the smooth capitalist system, rather than allowing them to remain awkward individuals. I think this is mostly untrue, and American post-war psychoanalysis is profound and fecund, and still worth reading.

Psychoanalysis has always claimed that it should not have a political view, and it is interesting that its greatest practitioners – Freud, Jung, Klein, Lacan – were all conservatives. But there are many liberal and left-wing psychoanalysts as well; and there is a long tradition of critical and anti-capitalist bias in psychoanalysis, which can work as a critique of capitalist convention.

Psychoanalysis is not a cure-all. It doesn't suit everyone, and it might be difficult to find an analyst who is right for you. I didn't shop around for my analyst, he was recommended by a friend; I just went to see him, he was starting out and he had a space. The moment I left my first session, I thought, this is for me, I want to be in this room with him, talking.

I've never regretted the time and money analysis has cost me, and it is certainly expensive. The French psychoanalyst Jacques Lacan wanted it to be. He believed that the more you paid, the more it hurt, and the more you'd benefit from it. There had to be a cost. Lacan didn't want you lying on the couch for months talking crap and being evasive. If he thought you were doing that, he'd cut short the session and invite you to leave. This method really hurried things along, but he was, despite these strange habits, a brilliant listener. In contrast, my analyst is a Freudian, and I wouldn't want to visit a Lacanian, though I have many Lacanian friends. I like knowing how long my session will be, and that I have an apportioned time slot. This means that I can lie down and say what I like, or stay silent if I want. In one session, I spent the whole time describing a long dream, and when I got to the end, with about thirty seconds to go, I asked my analyst what it meant. 'That is the story of your life,' he said.

My analyst has many writers on his books, and is a considerable writer himself. His patients continue to see him for many years. These particular analyst/patient relationships have lasted longer than many marriages, or other relationships. So this is an odd experiment. What happens if you extend a treatment over thirty years? What kind of analysis is this? And what is going on between therapist and patient?

My analyst knows me better than anyone else. I've spent more time with him than I did with my parents, a thought that always makes me laugh, because we are still talking about them. I wouldn't say that my analyst and I are friends; I don't want to be his friend, and I never ask him about himself, his opinions on football or politics. We do discuss literary topics, Kafka, Dostoevsky and Proust, which can be illuminating, and other times he knows I am evading a crucial issue. Some problems have remained for months on end, and I felt dead at the end of our sessions, as if I were trying to bury him under my depression. He said once, 'I am very tenacious. I will never give up.' I found this uplifting, despite the darkness of this particular period. But therapy always moves you on.

Psychoanalysis is not just a talking cure, or even a listening one. When you get out of that room you have to act; you must change your life; forming new relationships, speaking differently, altering your appearance, leaving people and making dramatic decisions. It is what happens outside the room that matters. You have to take risks, since everything you're doing is already a risk.

Psychoanalysis has been and still is – with its ideas about sexuality, gender and all the rest – at the centre of our culture, just as it has been for the last hundred years. Turn on the radio, and you will hear politicians and commentators talking about gender, the mystery of it, and how one becomes gendered and what it means to be a male or a female.

This is my last night here. I am leaving tomorrow for Stanmore.

04/10/2023

ROYAL NATIONAL ORTHOPAEDIC
HOSPITAL, STANMORE

Finally, I have moved from West London to a spinal rehab facility in North London. This is my fifth hospital since my accident, and I hope it will be my last. Like all these moves, it is disturbing and upsetting; you have to get used to a new room, and another set of nurses, doctors and physios. You must deal with people every day that you would never run into in the normal course of your life. This is both pleasurable and difficult. You must make conversation, even when you don't want to. Most of the people you meet in hospital are interested in your welfare, but still, you have to negotiate with them, which can be frustrating and enervating.

I have already made a friend, Jon, who is in a bay down the corridor, which he shares with three other people. It is much worse for him than it is for me in my single side room. There are disturbances all night: radios, nurses coming in and out, groans and the cries of the upset. He's lucky if he gets four hours' sleep.

He's woken up at six, which is when the nurses turn the lights on.

Jon had his accident in June while rock climbing. He fell on his head and broke his neck as well as both arms. He is a philosophy lecturer in London. It was a relief for both of us to share our complaints. Like me, he hates the mornings when the nurses wash you, dress you and work on your bowel with their fingers. He still finds it humiliating and degrading, which I do not because I have no dignity left to injure. But he is in his mid-thirties and had a lot of living still to do. He told me that he is often suicidal since it is almost unbearable to live with such loss. At the same time he talks about getting out of here and finding a new flat where he will be able to live alone as a semi-paralysed man.

He comes to talk to me in his motorized wheelchair but he is not allowed to enter my room because of my hospital bug. A nurse yelled at him, so he had to park himself outside and shout towards me sitting in bed. This I find more humiliating than any number of fingers up my arse. I am also banned from the day room, but I sneak in and hope no one is watching. It's a stark, dismal space, with plywood tables to eat at, and a large TV on the wall which is usually showing *Married at First Sight Australia*. There is a shelf of well-pawed beach reads and a couple of armchairs for visitors, and it is one of the few places on the ward where patients can meet and talk, but I worry all the time that I will be caught and thrown out. This hospital can feel like a prison, and I wonder again how I will stand it.

Jon and I discuss how boring it is to be in hospital. Hours and hours pass when there is nothing to do. But in this regard he is better off than me. He at least can watch television or read, though his hands, like mine, are pretty useless. I can listen to the radio but by now I have mastered the art of doing nothing. I can sit in my wheelchair and stare at a blank wall for two hours at a time. Occasionally I fall asleep or entertain myself with stories from my past or writing ideas. Jon distracts himself with sexual fantasies but I tell him that this is something of a losing game because nothing can come of it.

Isabella comments, 'You really know how to cheer people up.'

This new rehab is a long way from my friends and family in London. To get here, they must take the Jubilee Line to the last station, where a minibus will take them up the hill to the hospital. The ward is always difficult for visitors to find, since the hospital is sprawling and a bit of a maze. Some visitors have come all this way, got lost and returned home without seeing me.

It is an old military hospital which has been turned into a modern rehab facility with a well-equipped gym, swimming pool, coffee shop, and a lovely garden with elevated flower beds designed for people in wheelchairs. Isabella comes every day, and I have another friend, Samreen, who lives ten minutes away, and gives me face and head massages in the evenings.

Jon and I were discussing the loyalty of various friends and family members; those who visited once or twice and never came again, for instance. You like to be near the centre of others' attention but of course people in hospital are easily forgotten, with good reason, as there is only so much suffering that anyone can bear.

It was consoling to learn that Jon has the same obsessive thoughts that I do. Why has this happened to me? Why was I picked out for this misfortune when others are skipping down the street and living good lives? What would I do if I could go back in time? And why didn't I appreciate it more when I could use my hands and legs? It is boring. No wonder he wants to die.

14/10/2023

The world was always a dangerous place. This ward of the hospital is full of people who have had accidents. There are none, so far as I know, with degenerative diseases like MS. So there is a lot of talk about human misfortune: haphazard, calamitous, and near-fatal mishaps. You would think, staying on this ward, that everyone in the world was a moment or so from being, for instance, run over by a car, or struck by lightning, which happened to a friend of a friend, a man who was killed by a bolt on the way to his wedding.

After visiting me, another friend went home to Paris to prepare for a theatre show which was about to open. She stood on a chair to water some plants, and it almost goes without saying that she took a tumble and snapped her arm, which she had to carry to hospital, where she lay on a trolley for eight hours before she was operated on. Her show was cancelled. Another friend stepped out into the path of a cyclist who then crashed into her. The severely injured cyclist is taking legal action against my friend. These are only recent occurrences.

In here, there is much talk of contingency, of what might happen when you are not thinking about where your body is, when you are watering your plants, or walking down the street. There are injured surfers and many cyclists, some of them young; motorcyclists and car accident victims as well as two men who had disasters on trampolines. Swimming pools are dangerous if they are emptied overnight. There are many people who have fallen down the stairs. You are lucky to survive going to bed – one patient here fell out and broke his neck.

If you don't want to be severely injured or killed, avoid bathrooms, stairs, kitchens, gardens and the street.

I met a huge clever man in Rome who had fallen heavily down the stairs and it had taken him three years to learn to walk again. He told me that now he could walk one hundred and eighty steps and was proud of himself. I envy him that many steps. At the moment I can stand up in a hoist for about twenty minutes, but I cannot take any steps at all, and I wonder if I ever will. I would like to walk again, but my main priority is trying to get my hands moving. I can move a computer mouse a few inches, but otherwise I am reliant on other people for all the things you need to do with your hands, of which, I've begun to notice, there are many.

I am nervous now for my friends and family all the time. They are not aware, nor should they be, that at any moment, their present life could be over, if they slipped in the shower, or if they got hit by a reckless motorist. It is not something you should worry about; it is easier to live without increasing your burden of petty concerns. But as I say, living in the hospital of accidents teaches you that random evil stuff can happen to you at any time. The world is a killing machine – the simplest move could turn out to be fatal.

This time last year, in October, three months before my accident, I was a happy-go-lucky, innocent person, swinging about the world, enjoying myself, and complaining cheerfully.

Now, since I fainted while sitting in a chair –
rather than while sitting on the sofa or lying in
bed, which would have been more convenient –
I am a near-vegetable, and am denied the
pleasures that were in store for me. This has
changed the way I view the world. I now feel
anger and spite towards it. The other day, I was
trying to become religious; I wanted to set up a
relationship with God. God, I thought, would
be a great person to hate for all this; he could
take the blame; it would be his fault, and it
would focus my anger. But I wasn't convinced.
I couldn't hold the belief together. God wasn't
there. I couldn't wish him into being.

So an accident is just an accident. It is
truly contingent. There is no meaning to it.
You cannot think yourself around it. I love
the fact that the silent films I grew up watching as a kid – Buster Keaton, Charlie Chaplin,
Laurel and Hardy, and so on – were made
not so long after Freud wrote his great book
The Psychopathology of Everyday Life. Freud
seemed to find meaning in mistakes and accidents; they expressed unconscious desire. But I

don't believe my friend who stood on the chair to water her plants was unconsciously trying to have her show cancelled – however, I may be wrong about that.

The kind of accident I am talking about does not involve unconscious intention; not the slightest bit of it. And that is the problem with accidents – sometimes they are really just that: random, inexplicable mishaps. There is no accounting for them. No one to blame.

21/10/2023

Paki, writer, cripple: who am I now? Questions around identity have been among the most important and confusing of our day. Some are appalled that our society is being divided up into tiny tribes where people with a few common characteristics create identarian units. Surely this isn't strange, particularly in a culture as atomized and accelerated as ours. You like to be with people who are like you. It is defensive as well as reassuring.

The first time I was aware that I had an identity, and that it could be useful, was when I decided as a teenager that I wanted to be a writer. I started to call myself, in my mind, *a writer*. No one else knew that I was a writer because I hadn't written much and they certainly hadn't read it. But the notion that I could put this identity on like a new set of clothes, or a suit of armour, really helped me out. As a child and young man, I suffered racial abuse; I was at times, at school and on the street, known as 'Paki'. Calling myself a writer was a self-designation which protected me. If I hadn't yet become a writer, I would become one – it was an ambition, it made a future, and I wouldn't be the first person to take on a moniker long before they were ready to inhabit it. I can see the point and use of names.

I would walk about the city trying out phrases like 'Meet Hanif Kureishi, he's a writer' or 'This is Hanif Kureishi, have you read his books?' I liked the sound of that. I've been a writer continually since then, and I've never grown less fond of the designation. It got me places. But since my accident I have become more of a patient than a writer. I am a patient all day, a more or less anonymous body to the nurses who take care of me. I can feel my identity slipping, as if I am forgetting who I am and becoming someone else, or almost nothing. I never thought my identity would be scrubbed out or superseded by something else.

My imagination feels muted. I have lost my spark a bit. My circumstances have become so strange that I can't locate an idea of myself. I can't write fiction – stories, movies or novels – because my condition is so urgent that inhabiting other worlds feels impossible.

It is odd to think that as I sit in this bleak hospital room, things are, in other respects, going well. The Curve Theatre in Leicester is reviving its excellent production of *My Beautiful Laundrette*, which will tour around northern towns early next year. At the same time, the Royal Shakespeare Company is developing an adaptation of my first novel, *The Buddha of Suburbia*, which will rehearse in the spring, and open at the Swan, Stratford, before coming to London.

This writing I have done in hospital, dictated to Carlo and my family, has sustained me. I want to keep going. I often despair, but unlike Jon, I have no wish to die. Out of horror, something new must arise.

I will have a new identity – an additional one, I guess – as a disabled person, something which I am not prepared for yet. It isn't a welcoming designation. I don't want to be seen like that, and yet I may well have to get used to it, which is a conflict for me. My house is already being altered for my return. This is real. It had to be done. And so, if I was ever tempted to think of all this as a dream, the workers currently disturbing Isabella in the house make it clear that this is reality.

28/10/2023

I wasn't much cop as a stage manager on the touring production of Kafka's *Metamorphosis*. I was far too disorganized, always losing things and in a panic. What I really wanted to be was a playwright. But Steven Berkoff, who directed the production, was generous with me; I became his letter writer and sideman for a few months before Erica Bolton got me a job at Riverside Studios, working for David Gothard and Peter Gill. This meant that I got to see Kafka's *Metamorphosis* on many occasions, in different theatres, as we travelled around in a van. Often now, lying helplessly on my back, I think of Kafka's beetle or insect – what a rich metaphor it is, and how it works on as many levels as you like. I recall how repulsed and angry Gregor Samsa's family and other visitors are with him. As his health deteriorates, he is found to be disgusting, and I believe towards the end of the story he is pelted with apples.

I was discussing this with my analyst on my

weekly call, and we were saying that in reality, when you have an accident, suddenly becoming disabled, you find that the people around you are immensely sympathetic. They want to help you. They love to give you things; they rush to your side. They imagine how they might feel if they were in your situation, how they would want to be loved. Kafka is a pessimistic writer; his view of the world will always resonate, but I have found my friends and family, and even people I barely know, to be compassionate. They write letters, send presents, come to visit, and sometimes make extravagant financial offers, which, in the future, I may have to take them up on.

It has been odd to spend so much of my recent life, to share so many intimate events, with strangers. Only this morning, a young female doctor put a finger up my arse to test how responsive my rectum was. I meet more people here in a week than I did in a year in my previous life. I have met scores of nurses, doctors and physios in the last year. I have learned that it is a good idea to be kind and polite with people who are trying to help. I strive not to be grumpy, though I can hear myself being irritable and old-mannish.

It is easy to talk to people. If you want, with a few simple enquiries, you can trigger a tsunami of confession. Lying on my bed, in the evening, while being changed, I can unlock terrible and unsettling stories. Many are bizarre and outlandish; tales from asylums, accounts of kidnap, and other forms of violence and emotional terror.

People like to talk; they want to tell you about themselves; they want you to know them. It can be overwhelming; too much of it is difficult to take in. I ask my analyst, and other therapist friends, how it is they can listen all day to disturbing things. But it is their work; they have chosen to do it, they know how to protect themselves. As a writer, I am curious about the dramatic lives of others: you would think I would welcome these responses. But I require more distance – I had it in my previous life, and it suited me. I met friends where and when I wanted. There would be a limit to what I would have to put up with; I could control it. But now I am here, and wanting to be kind, I ask these new people simple questions, which at times can trigger an avalanche of disclosure. I hear things I want to forget quickly. This is not a pub, people tend not to tell you things that are cheerful; you don't hear many jokes. I was speaking to one patient, a taxi driver, who picked up a suitcase at the airport and broke his spine in two; another kid, a friendly and lively boy who whips up and down the corridor in his wheelchair, was disabled after being tasered by the police.

Hospital workers can be overly optimistic: they like to tell you that you are making progress; they want to feel that their work isn't futile. But I am aware, even as they tell me all this, that I am still a broken man with a smashed body.

The nurses here are from all over the world. Their stories have a universal resonance, and are told in a variety of accents; there are Filipinos, Indians, South Africans, West Indians and many from Ghana and Nepal. There is much talk in British politics about cutting down on immigration, but as we know, the British people want two things at once: an efficient, fully-staffed NHS, and less immigration. The NHS and the care homes only survive on a constant influx of immigration, and I've noticed, being in hospital so long, how many new immigrants there are, people who have come to the UK recently on working visas.

One thing that has changed in my life this year is that I get to spend much more time with people that I know. Tracey said to me the other day that she sees me far more now than she ever did. Every morning I call my sons and family on FaceTime. Samreen visits me a few times a week, to bring me food, a headscratcher and now a backscratcher. She and I are able to hang out for much longer than we would normally. Sitting in a pub, the meeting would usually go on for no longer than ninety minutes, and we might not see each other for months afterwards. This emergency has created a space for more complex friendships.

I am doing physiotherapy every day. I can stand for about twenty minutes with physios either side of me, or in a standing machine, which holds me from the front and back. I do not have the strength to take a step, so I cannot think about walking. The occupational therapists have been working on my hands, but I still cannot grip anything, brush my teeth, feed myself, or pick up a pen. I feel stronger in my body, but my wheelchair has given me a sore arse, so I am spending a lot of time in bed, bored out of my mind. I have an electric wheelchair now, which means I am more independent and can get around the ward, nudging the joystick with my right hand, even though I can't use my fingers. I go into the day room and out into the garden, if it is not raining. As I say, though, sitting for long periods, with my body weight on my arse, is not something I've got used to.

I have been told that I will leave here on December 20th, to go home, where I will need care and attention for much of the day. Across the corridor, I can see the nurses chatting. I will miss the security they give me, being always available.

4/11/2023

Two nurses were discussing me as they worked this morning, one saying to the other, 'He's the man who never smiles.' I replied, 'No one says anything remotely funny.' It is true, I am not a man who smiles easily; I don't like being made to laugh. But comedy is my favourite form. I like to make others laugh, and am often accused of having a dry sense of humour.

Sometimes I'm asked why I put humour in my books, but to me that is like asking why you write a book with a story. The humour is integral to the idea and the language, just as it might be integral to a person, the way they speak and view the world.

My father was an amusing man. One of his favourite writers was Oscar Wilde. Dad loved *wit*, but, like me, he didn't much like being told jokes, which he found cumbersome. Wit is spontaneous, it comes out of a particular situation, it is not planned or calculated, but occurs in the moment as a surprise and shock; it is sudden and alters the atmosphere.

My father was funny all day, and his brothers, of whom there were many, were similar; humour rippled through them. Anything could be amusing, and should be, that was the point of conversation; the reason for people to interact was to cheer one another up. They would make each other laugh, but seemingly without calculation. It came naturally.

Anything can be amusing: my son Carlo reminded me that in Primo Levi's great books about Auschwitz, the characters, despite their dire situation, or perhaps because of it, still try to amuse one another.

This is odd for me to write, because I must admit that I don't much like laughter. When people laugh near me, particularly in this hospital, it annoys me; I feel like saying, 'What the fuck is so funny in this shithole that you can laugh like that?' It makes me want to strangle them.

This injury has made me envious, particularly of other people's pleasures, and maybe, when they are laughing, I sense that they are enjoying a happiness that eludes me. But I do think that almost all the great writers are essentially comic: Shakespeare, Dickens, Proust, Joyce, and of course Kafka – anyone apart from Tolstoy, who could be earnest, and not known for his humour. Humour is a bulwark against boredom, and boredom, especially in hospital, is the most corrosive thing there is. This year in hospital, I've been bored more than you can imagine. Hours have passed where nothing has happened, where I have just been lying in bed, waiting for a shower, waiting for Isabella to turn up, waiting for distraction, listening to the horrible news over and over.

Oddly enough, I haven't lost my sense of humour, despite my miserable demeanour. I am visited here, in my room, by a serious NHS psychiatrist (I wonder if there has ever been a humorous psychiatrist). Foolishly, I like to try to make him laugh, to see if I can break through the skin of his professionalism. He is staid and likes telling me I am clinically depressed. His single solution with me, and

I guess other patients, is to prescribe more anti-depressants. I suppose this will make him feel less useless.

I understand as we talk that psychiatrists are not therapists; they are not so interested in listening, and they diagnose too soon, as if that is all they are concerned with. They don't appear to want to know more about what is going on. That is what annoys me. But despite everything, the psychiatrist continues to visit me, and I've ended up analysing his dreams. Since he was struck by how often he dreams about Donald Trump, I had to inform him of how much he envies Trump's brutality and freedom to do or say whatever occurs to him.

Sometimes I try to do the same thing to the doctors, to get past their enactment of a particular role, to see if there is something softer underneath, something I can reach, which will reveal whether they are more than a talking medical encyclopaedia.

Freud wrote an entire book about jokes in which there are not many jokes, and the ones he did include are not funny. He recognized that humour, like sexuality, is where we can be taken by surprise, and where the unconscious exposes itself. The unconscious is not quite underneath; it is more like something which is subtly hidden in plain sight, but can be unlocked with the keys of humour or desire, and of course the two are closely related. Wit is the brilliant expression of a truth, a way of exposing something with concision and effect, making the world seem like a brighter place. After all, much of the entertainment that we consume in movies, on TV, in literature and via social media is comedic in some form or another. We are the animals looking for laughs.

When I saw my uncles and their friends trying to amuse and outwit one another, I knew I wanted to be like that when I grew up. If I am funny, in conversation, it is something I had to learn and cultivate; it is a form of creativity, as is all conversation.

11/11/2023

A young writer once asked me why it was so difficult to write about sex. I answered glibly that all writing was difficult. Writing about marriage, death, landscapes, historical characters, or whatever, none of it was easy. Nor should it be easy. There should be some friction in your method, between you and your subject matter. Think how crazy it would be if you could just sit down and write a masterpiece followed by another masterpiece. Frustration and difficulty are integral to the process. But I also regretted my reply to the young writer because now, looking back, it is obvious that there was more to be said.

It is difficult to write about sex, just as it is difficult to write about music; the sensations are so intimate and intense, it is hard to find a vocabulary to suit the occasion. Words like 'member', 'thrust' or 'cried out', etc., always sound banal, if not ridiculous, when compared to the complexity of the sexual situation, where there is so much going on.

It seems odd that in the 1950s and 60s, when I was growing up, no one was allowed to write explicitly about sex. In those days, books were still censored or prosecuted. There were trials for Henry Miller, Nabokov and of course D. H. Lawrence, all of whom attempted to write about copulation – from a male perspective, of course. It is absurd that such harmless works were ever considered dangerous. Now, anyone can write what they like about sex, and no one will complain, at least in the West. But perhaps another sort of repression has been established by making sex banal or mundane; it has perhaps lost the charge and meaning it once had. But that might just be me, because of my injury, with sex now seeming to exist in an alternative universe, or solely in the past.

Last night, here in the hospital, I was talking to my promiscuous, bisexual friend with prostate cancer. Looking back, he was amazed by how much of his life had been taken up by sex:

fantasizing about it, planning it, shopping for it, deceiving, lying, doing it and recalling it. He even took up with a male prostitute who, two weeks after being with my friend – and having robbed him – then killed one of his other clients by drug overdose. He and I discussed why sex had meant so much to us as a generation, and wondered how we should think about it now. It was as though we had been possessed, and when the fever had gone, we could only speculate what it had all been about.

Literature has always dealt with sexuality. It has been there, but subtly and disguised. You find it in the theatre, from Shakespeare to Tennessee Williams, buried in the language. I was only thinking the other day about how much sex there is in the second part of *Middlemarch*, a novel not usually celebrated for its eroticism.

What a shame it is, and also an absurdity, that there has not been more explicit sexuality in great literature. I would have loved to have learned what the characters we are most fond of liked to do in bed: what they wore, what they said, how they behaved, what their kinks and fetishes were. Freud told us that sexuality was at our centre. That seems something of an exaggeration now. We are more likely to say that violence is at the core of our souls and our civilizations. But still, I would have relished the opportunity to hear from the masters – Tolstoy, Chekhov or E. M. Forster – what they could have told us about sex, had they been free to write without inhibition.

What a wasted opportunity it was that for centuries the public and their censors were unable to bear writing or reading about the activity of copulation. There are marginalized sexualities, particularly gay and lesbian preferences, which have been doubly repressed. We could have learned so much about pleasure and desire if we had not been so afraid of a writer describing an orgasm. If sexuality is such a driving and defining aspect of human behaviour, it seems a mystery that it has been so excluded from literary description. Sexual censorship seems absurd now, which isn't to say it doesn't exist still in a good deal of the world.

It is true, and there is no doubt, that sex is

difficult to write about. The vocabulary is often impoverished; it is like trying to trap music or water in language: you have to be delicate, and you'd probably be better off describing the act from the inside, from the character's point of view, what each action means to them, and why they wanted to do it. After all, sexuality is as individual as any other act, like conversation or laughter, and to describe a character fully in a play or a novel, you'd probably want to have an idea of what they like to do in bed. That would tell you a great deal about them. How could you leave such a thing out? What a motivating factor it is, particularly when you are young.

Since it has generally been impossible to explicitly present sexuality in novels, films and plays, artists, writers and directors have had to find creative ways of portraying these acts. You can sense it in Shakespeare's sonnets, which as we know are soaked in carnality. You might argue that leaving sexuality out creates a sense of mystery. But censorship, even though it may inspire creative solutions, is never to be welcomed. If we abolish sexuality in literature, we lose something that drives us, that makes us love and laugh. Our desires confuse and amaze us; they are forces so powerful that I can see why they may need to be hidden. But my view is that sexuality should be celebrated, explored and protected, since it is something that makes us both creative and fascinated by others.

Before the internet, when I was writing short pornographic stories for top-shelf magazines, I'd imagine the readers would be more interested in the pictures than in my little written sketches. But in those days, unpublished young writers like me could supplement their dole money by churning out filth. These stories would often involve bored housewives seducing manual workers like plumbers or gardeners. (Why not architects?) This was a fundamental fantasy and it was repeated endlessly with the same words used over and over again. It was dull to write and boring to read. I guess we writers tried to make these pieces as original and lively as we could, but originality wasn't required: all you had to do was repeat a few trigger words to create excitement in the reader, who would then, presumably, jerk off. It seems funny now, if not a bit desperate, that people would turn to writing, rather than images, for stimulation.

In those days, I lived in a house with a basement, and as I wrote and rewrote my pieces, I would screw up the rewritten pages into a ball and throw them out of the window into the garden of the flat below. Later, I came to know the couple who lived downstairs, and the woman said to me that she had been horrified to open up these balled-out bits of typed paper and read such obscenities. She'd had a romanticized idea of writers and wondered whether I was something of a young Graham Greene living upstairs, rather than a purveyor of smut.

18/11/2023

You would have thought that with the end of my hospital stay in sight I would be more cheerful. And I am in fact reasonably chirpy. But as we approach the date when I am to leave, I have become more apprehensive.

I am concerned particularly for Isabella and the responsibilities that she will have to take on. She and my caseworker will have to arrange various forms of care, which, while I am here in hospital, is an around-the-clock procedure. The advantage of being in hospital is that I am surrounded by nurses and medical amenities. It will not be the same at home. When I think about it, I realize that I am barely capable of doing anything for myself. I will need to be got up in the morning, washed, dressed, and hauled out of bed and into my chair. It will be like raising the *Titanic*. Then I will require someone to feed me, take me to the shops, prepare lunch for me, and run various errands regarding my work and my job at the university, where I teach

creative writing. The extent of my helplessness is becoming clearer to me as I think of the
future.

I was discussing this with a fellow patient, a
middle-aged man who, earlier this year, was in
his garden when he turned and tripped over a
rake, breaking his neck. Now he is confined to
a wheelchair and can use only one hand. I am
impressed by his outrage. He complains about
the shock of what has happened to him, as if
it is a radical inconvenience. One day he was
living his life, in what he calls a *normal way*, and
the next he had to find someone to wipe his arse
and help him out of bed. The violence of this
break with his former life shows on his face.
He will be leaving soon, but will require a carer
to live in his house. He will need another carer
when the first carer takes a break. He will have
to request constant assistance from the district
nurse and the council. This will be me too.

I am having a bathroom created in my living
room, and part of the wall in my hall is being
deconstructed to create space for my wheelchair
and possibly for a stairlift which I may or may

not have installed in the future. For Isabella, this work – the dust and noise – is a huge bother. She had never expected to be living in a house constructed for a disabled person, where all the equipment for incapacitated life is crammed together in a relatively small space.

In hospital, I am spared all of this, but I am hoping that the work will be done before I get back. My life and that of my family has taken a nasty turn. This is not a pleasurable semi-retirement. No one in the family can avoid being caught up in this tragedy. We have all had to adapt and overcome our resistance to change.

Meanwhile I move around the hospital in my electric wheelchair. I can drive from my room to the day room, where people eat and watch TV; or I can go out into the garden room and chat with the volunteers. Then I can take a spin around the garden itself, if it is not too cold or raining. I do a loop, return to my room and listen to the radio. It is a small world I exist in, but I am used to it now, and I am nervous of leaving it.

This place I occupy is inhabited by disabled

people and their carers. Being semi-immobilized here is not such a big deal. People do not talk down to you. But becoming a disabled person in an able-bodied world is another matter. I fear the eyes of others, and what they will think when they see me. I dread my fantasies about what healthy and exciting lives they lead in their fit bodies. I will never be like them again; I will have to learn how to inhabit who I have become. But I do not wish to, there is a struggle in me, I do not want to give up my former self.

02/12/2023

My world has both shrunk and expanded. I am doing new things every day, things I never imagined for a moment. I am living in a small room off the main thoroughfare of a hospital ward, which houses twenty-eight patients. If I sit in my electric wheelchair at the entrance to my room, I am directly opposite the nurses' station, at which three or four nurses are usually doing different tasks. The patients roll up and down the drag, along with visitors, doctors, nurses, porters, agency workers, and so on. I am right in the middle of this busy ecosystem, overhearing all kinds of conversation. I am, as they say, watching the world go by, and it is not without interest. Sometimes there are two or three hours when I have no visitors or physio sessions, and I cannot, for practical reasons, watch a movie or read a book, so all I do is stare and listen.

When it is time to leave my room and go to my session in the gym, which is about five minutes across the hospital from here, I will greet many of the nurses and doctors, who I now know by name.

Yesterday I ran into Jon. He was coming towards me in his wheelchair looking more depressed and hangdog than ever, even for him. 'I just shat myself,' he said.

'How did that happen?' I said. 'I thought the nurses emptied your bowels this morning?'

'Yes,' he said, 'so did I.'

To cheer him up, I tell him that I pissed myself earlier that day, because my catheter tube got twisted as I was hoisted into my chair. I had to have my trousers changed. Jon is paralysed from the tits down, and so he can shit himself at any moment, having no control over his lower body. He worries that if he goes back to work as a teacher he could have an accident while lecturing. Along with this, he has many other concerns, like where he will live when he leaves this hospital. Other patients here, some of whom are still in their twenties, are in the same position. When they finally have to leave, unless there is suitable accommodation for them, they will be put into a care home, at least for a while, until somewhere better is arranged. It could take months. The problem with care homes is that there is little or no physio available, and certainly no gym. I am the lucky one, with a house to return to, and a partner and family who will support me.

As I move further down the corridor, a man in a wheelchair stops me, asking if I am Hanif. I guess he is in his mid-thirties, in a bright track-suit with a youthful vigour and a lot of energy in his arms as he skids about the place. A few years ago he was a patient here. His accident was dramatic: while staying in a hotel abroad, a terrorist attack occurred. Hearing shooting outside his room, he opened his door to find the building was on fire. He attempted to escape by tying his bedsheets together and climbing out of the window. He fell and broke his back. He has, what they call here, a 'complete break'. He tells me all of this, as I guess he tells other patients, to make a connection with us, so that we can see how far he has come, from a miserable start in 2009. He says he wishes he had written it all down, as I did, when it occurred, capturing the raw feeling of the moment, the exact horror experienced, without reflection. Otherwise you forget the details; there is no way you can remember it all.

As I continue down the corridor, past the bays on the left, I smell dope, and know that the kids, the young patients, have been smoking again. The nurses rush about berating these sad and charming boys, who are much liked by the staff here for their cheek and verve. Then there is the long corridor which leads to the gym. As I look out, there are trees and grass, and I reflect on how far away I feel from my family. When I head into the gym, I recognize everyone there: the physios and the occupational therapists, the students and the new patients.

It is lunchtime, and I have nothing of my own to eat in the fridge, which means I'll be eating hospital food, macaroni cheese, the one thing on the menu I am able to consume without wanting to throw up. The nurse slips my left arm into a metal sling called a 'de-weighter' which enables it to be suspended. A specially designed fork is stuck into my splint, so that I can grab a piece of macaroni and lift it to my mouth. This is, as you can imagine, a time-consuming and inaccurate process. I get some of the macaroni cheese in my mouth, but a lot of it goes down my front, and some of it ends up on the floor. Whichever way I eat, it is a nightmare: if I am being fed by someone else, the delivery of the food is always at the wrong rate, too slow or too quick, and I am aware that I am utterly dependent on another person. But the nurse wants me to be, as she puts it, 'independent', so that when I leave here I will be able to feed myself. It all seems futile: the act of delivering food into your mouth is only a small fraction of the eating procedure; I cannot walk to the shops or take things out of the fridge, use kitchen appliances or do the washing-up.

Three of the physios take me to a hydrotherapy pool at the other end of the hospital. One of them plays some Mozart through his phone while the other two change into swimming costumes. I am then strapped to a chair and lowered into the warm water. Floating on my back, I am pulled about the pool by the two physios. It is a lovely experience; I relax, kicking my legs and moving my arms. I want to stretch out and swim. Then I sit down on a ledge at the end of the pool, stand up, and take a few steps. Underwater, movement is easy, and I find that I can actually walk, I can move my legs forward and tread the length of the small pool without getting tired. I am exhilarated and optimistic; I want to be doing this all the time.

09/12/2023

I wish nothing in my world had changed. But there have been interesting alterations. One of those has been my relationships with the women in my life, who have come to care for me in a more intimate and extended way.

When I first had my accident, and was still in Rome, and then in the two London hospitals, I hated to be alone at all, and I had many visitors: family, friends, acquaintances, and people I have worked with. But some relationships developed in ways I could never have anticipated, just as my demands for tenderness and friendship have developed. Samreen still comes in at least once a week, though she has her own family, bringing me food and massaging my hands; we spend hours together, talking about politics, dreams, schools, Shakespeare and anything else that occurs to us. She and I have been friends for years – I taught her writing at one point – but previously would meet only occasionally to exchange information about our lives. Now I need much more from her as well as from other people, and I have received it, with additions.

Another woman, who I was not so close to before, but who has suffered a lot in her life, now brings me food, sits with me for two or three hours, and reads the newspapers aloud to me. She will then clean my teeth, lay my clothes out for the next day, lower my head and put me to bed, helping to prepare me for the night. Almost everyone who has visited me asks the same question: 'Is there anything I can do?' Well, yes, there is plenty, if you really want to help.

People have been doing things that I could never have imagined needing help with before: having my pyjamas changed, head scratched, being available for long conversations, and just sitting here while I doze. Other friends whom I would have only seen every couple of months have been visiting every day, in some cases. In the previous two hospitals, Isabella says it got a little crazy, with people coming in and out at all times of the day. There were some odd meet-ups, and some interesting ones, in my cramped little room on the dementia ward. Two movie directors discussing how they prefer digital to film, because it is simpler to revise – you can relight a scene in the cutting room. A psychoanalyst, sex therapist and a pop singer, discussing why children won't go to school these days. A novelist and one of my sons chatting about social media and attention spans. A former banker brought me two bottles of Bollinger, much filthy political gossip and a VR headset, to cheer me up.

Isabella wondered, as mentioned earlier, whether it was getting too busy, and whether people were just coming to look at me, like some kind of curiosity. But I had had insomnia, was feeling alone and depressed, and these meetups with unexpected combinations of people were a reminder that there was still a world to be interested in. My visitors are a connection to a country I fear losing touch with.

It is remarkable what my injury has evoked in other people; what it has brought out in them. I wonder who I am for them, what I mean to them, but perhaps this is not something I can grasp, or that they can know. A condition such as mine, in which vulnerability is so central, clearly touches something in people, and I have found them to be truly devoted. But sometimes this worries me, because I wonder if I would be able to do the same for others. I don't know that I would; I doubt I would, but I just don't know. Obviously I feel differently about illness now. I don't see it so much as an intrusion, but as an inevitable and essential part of life, particularly as we live longer.

My relationship with my partner, Isabella, and with Tracey has also changed. They do far more for me than I can do for them, and I wonder what I will be able to do in the future to equalize things a little, as if that were necessary. Do relationships have to be equal? My female friends have gone further in their care than the men; they are more physical, nourishing and openly loving and they are less afraid of illness and hospitals than their male counterparts. When they arrive they always tidy up.

My bond with my three boys has also developed in ways I hadn't expected. Sachin was angry with me for a while; he would sit in my hospital room vibrating with fury about my condition; he couldn't wait to get out and go home to get on with his life, as if I were an obstacle. And then sometimes he would return an hour later feeling guilty and annoyed with himself. But if I ever wondered why anyone would want to have children at all, I can assure you that it will pay off in the long run, and that they will love you as you loved them when they were helpless and dependent. I am saying all of this because someone asked me the other day whether I thought anything good had come out of this catastrophe. I disliked the question because I didn't want to credit this horror with any progress. But I have had to learn to make demands of the people around me; I cannot worry if I am inconveniencing them, and if I do, they have to tell me, so a new channel of communication has opened up in me: I cannot hide my thoughts or wishes, I've had to learn how to ask. I guess I like to believe that I was a relatively inhibited person, who didn't want to be a nuisance, but all of this is subterfuge or false; sometimes being direct is the only way through.

I certainly worried at the beginning whether this accident would render me weaker and less powerful as a father, partner or friend. But I am in fact more powerful now as a sick person. The sick can dominate a family, sucking out all the oxygen. To be sick is sometimes to have a stranglehold over others; because of your condition they cannot refuse you, and they might feel that their demands can't rival yours.

16/12/2023

Skidding down the ward in my electric wheel-chair, I am in a slightly more buoyant mood than usual since I am supposedly leaving here in a couple of days. I run into Jon, who, like me, read philosophy at university, and I ask him if he has a moment to discuss a pressing moral issue.

One of my sons attended a small party recently, and as a generous gift took two chocolate bars containing magic mushrooms, leaving them in a bag at the entrance. It should go without saying that within a short space of time, the family dog had penetrated the bag, and had its way with the magic mushrooms, consuming most of them. Soon, the beast — which was a chihuahua — was tripping off its head, whimpering hysterically. The dog had to be rushed to the vet to have its stomach pumped, which not only added to the ruin of the evening but cost the host five hundred quid. The dog, eventually, was fine. The next morning, the host asked my son to pay the vet's bill. But whose responsibility was it? This was what the philosopher and I discussed. We both concluded, of course, that it was the host's duty to control their excitable chihuahua, particularly as the chocolate was well wrapped up.

Nevertheless, there was some wrangling between my son and the host as to who should pay the bill, but Jon was adamant: it was the owner's responsibility, unless it became a legal issue, when the magic mushrooms themselves, a banned drug, would then come into play.

We continued this thorny discussion as Jon was having his urine bag emptied. Before we parted, I asked him how he was proceeding with his plans to kill himself, another moral matter we had been considering. Because it is difficult to kill yourself while paralysed and in hospital, he had decided that the most effective method, and least painful, was to die of hypothermia in the garden. But as it is relatively mild now, I said he could be sitting out there for hours. He claimed that it would take twelve minutes to die dressed in a T-shirt. He must have googled it.

But the chances were that someone would see him, and he might be sectioned. Unfortunately, he would have to go on living, even over Christmas, which is now approaching.

Later, I saw coming towards me a young nurse who had been taking care of me. She was looking unusually cheerful. What had brought on this burst of sunshine? She told me she had got a new, better-paid job. She was tired of the long hours and low wages of her present occupation. She had applied and been accepted to become a prison officer in a women's jail not far from here. I congratulated her but said that the conditions would be tougher than they are on this ward, where things worked pretty well, and it was reasonably calm.

At the end of the 1980s, I worked briefly as a creative writing teacher at a women's prison, Holloway Park, in North London. I cannot forget the awful smell of the place, the cries and moans, and the clanking of the keys as the warders locked the doors behind you. The class was the most difficult I had taught. There were five or six women in it, most of whom, as far as I knew, were murderers. I tried to encourage them to write their stories but didn't know how literate or how dyslexic they were. Some of them had been in prison since their late teens, and one woman, notoriously, had stabbed her violent pimp to death. Sitting at the back of the class, as I tried to teach them about creativity and the therapy of writing, she would lift her shirt and wiggle her bare breasts at me. My attempts at teaching these troubled women ended when the other teacher I worked with, a young black playwright, was locked up by one of the warders, who accused her of trying to escape in plain clothes. It took some time for the authorities to be persuaded that this woman was an educationalist and not a criminal.

Today, in the gym, I am joined by a middle-aged African man, a stranger who is due to come and live in my house as my carer. I am a chatty person, and he is worryingly quiet, if not withdrawn. Soon I became exhausted trying to get anything out of him, except his complaint that he only liked to eat his own food, especially a yam at lunchtime. I said he'd be lucky to get a yam on the hospital menu, but it would be easier to get food that he liked when we are in West London.

I am becoming quite exercised by the issue of going home and living with a stranger as well as Isabella. But that is my situation now, after a year of all this. And not only that, it turns out that some of the equipment, like the hoist which the carer will use to get me in and out of bed, might not arrive until January.

Some of the patients, including my suicidal philosophical pal, will have to stay here over Christmas where there will be no physio or other therapies. I imagine that it will be bleak. The doctor tells me that I am welcome to stay, but I really don't fancy it.

18/12/2023

I am leaving today, but my carer has failed to turn up, and I worry about going home without support. Isabella will do her best, but she is not, and does not want to be, a professional carer.

And then, suddenly, I am in my wheelchair outside the ward entrance, preparing to be strapped into the back of a converted van. I have spent a year in five hospitals and I am finally going home. A woman has now arrived as the replacement carer and she seems charming and capable. Forty minutes later, I am at last in my own house. There is now a bed in my living room and a new downstairs bathroom with smart yellow tiles. I am agitated, elated, and confused, as I always am when entering a new situation – but mostly I am relieved.

20/12/2023

'Are you religious? How religious are you? Do you know what time it is? Is it day or night? Where are we? We need to find out how responsive you are.'

Five strangers are sitting around my dining-room table. These 'providers' are here to ascertain whether I will have my care package confirmed, and in what form. At present, I have a live-in carer, and another one who arrives twice a day to help get me in and out of bed. As we know, this government is determined to make tax cuts before the next election, which will be paid for by reducing social care for the vulnerable. I could be one of those cuts. In order not to be, Isabella and I have to demonstrate how needy and sick I am. I must dial up the distress, if possible, or there is a risk I may have to sell my house in order to get my arse wiped.

My house is in a busy district, but by some kind of good luck, it is more or less completely silent. Lying in bed on the ground floor, I can't hear a thing. By necessity, I am still in the hands of the medical system. I wake up at seven when my carer, a pleasant African woman who now lives at the top of the house, comes to wake me up, and my day begins with a suppository. Soon after, there is a loud banging at the front door when the local council sends another carer to assist with my washing and dressing. It is professional work, and each day a different young man comes to help. I am lifted out of bed and returned to bed according to the bureaucratic protocols of the NHS. I cannot choose when to rise or when to lie down.

There is a complicated and obscure etiquette when it comes to being looked after. In some areas the carer's duties are obvious: to deal with my bowel, bladder and catheter, to wash me, prepare my meds, get me in and out of bed and make my breakfast and coffee. But there are grey areas. Is it her work to mix me a Bloody Mary? To send texts to my friends, or make them a tea when they come round? She is a carer not a servant. Yet what choice do I have but to make demands, and discover whether they will be reciprocated?

My carers are all immigrants. Having lived and worked in a white world for the best part of forty years, most of my adult life, I am back where I began with my father, his family and friends, among people who have recently arrived and are not used to things here, as they strive to make lives for themselves and their children.

Every morning, I work with Carlo on fashioning my dispatches into this book. It is a pleasure to edit with someone else, as we cut, shape and expand the material. We start at ten in the morning and finish at one, getting about five pages of editing and rewriting done. It reminds me of collaborating on plays and movies with directors and dramaturgs, where there is plenty of amusing gossip about politics and sport, even as you work. It is consoling to spend time alone as a writer, but it is a blast to have companionship and banter.

Isabella's grandmother Suso Cecchi d'Amico, the screenwriter, said in an interview that the best way to write comedies was to work with others, since you can test the humour as you go. The internal critical voice, the one that tells you that you are no good, is muted when there are others to cheer you along. Writers can learn from musicians and movie people; both practices emerge out of creative alliances, from the Beatles to Miles Davis, Hitchcock to Robert Altman. Maybe the most important thing an artist can do is go to school with the right people, or have the ability to recognize a compatible talent. An artist can then do something they can't do alone. Would we have heard of Lennon or McCartney if they had never met? It is an enhancing and at times terrible dependency.

22/12/2023

Sachin has been away for a couple of weeks, and when he comes bouncing into the house, he seems to have grown. As a family we were never huge; Tracey and I are about the same size: five foot six. Sachin is wearing thick shoes, but he also seems to have got wider. As he is a twin, I can compare him to his brother, and he does seem to have got broader as well as taller.

It is a sunny late-December day, and we go out of the house and on to the Shepherd's Bush Road, me in my motorized wheelchair. As we pass Le Petit Citron, a French restaurant – formerly the notorious Café Rouge, where I was seen every night, carousing with friends – we are both struck by the same memory. About a year ago, Tracey and Carlo were watching a documentary about the band Nirvana and their first London tour. The band had the good fortune to be staying in a rough B&B on the Shepherd's Bush Road, and were filmed larking about outside the Rouge. The producer of the documentary had now returned to the scene, filming the Shepherd's Bush Road as it is today. By coincidence, they filmed Sachin barrelling into an establishing shot, and me crouching in the doorway of Le Petit Citron, ready to jump out at him. Because I am omnipresent in the area, Tracey and Carlo had in fact half-expected to see me – and so they did, and they cried with laughter.

It is difficult not to think of this as Sachin and I make our way up the road, but after a few yards, I am more concerned with the unevenness of the pavement. If you are newly in a wheelchair, you will be aware, for the first time in your life, of the exact nature of the street you are covering. You are closer to the ground than ever before; every bump shoots through you with a shock.

Things improve when we get to Shepherd's Bush Green, where the path is smoother. Soon we are outside my barber's, where a rough-looking man in a wheelchair rides up close to me and admires my chair, pointing out its features enviously and asking where I got it. I explain that it is the NHS's finest.

It has been more than a year since I have had a haircut from my constant barber, the Macedonian Lula, whom I consider to have the hands of Michelangelo. Our family have known him for fifteen years, since he was installed in a leaky shed next to a petrol station on the Goldhawk Road. Lula, in fact, gave Kier his first adult haircut, and the boys and I used to get shaved there. Now, Lula has two salons and a restaurant nearby, as well as a permanently worried look.

Sachin gets me over the threshold and into the shop where a space is made for my chair. Kier, my youngest son, joins us. It is a relief to be back doing normal things, on a regular day, in my hood. Often all four of us would be in the barber's together: gossiping, listening to music, arguing over who goes first, and trying to avoid one of Lula's fresh recruits who would inevitably give you the 'Serbian Rapist Look'.

During Covid, when you weren't allowed to fraternize, the boys and I would have to get haircuts surreptitiously. We would meet around the back of Lula's building, passing through an anonymous door, along several damp corridors, and into a room where we'd never been before, with no windows. We would sit before a minuscule mirror the size of an iPhone screen, illuminated by a single bulb, while Lula would get to work with his scissors. It was as if we were part of an underground resistance movement, or doing a drug deal.

Now, looking out of the window, across the Green, I see someone I recognize. It is the father of one of Kier's friends. When Kier was at primary school, he came home one day after playing with this man's son, and announced that he had become a Muslim. I found him on his knees praying in front of the television, and he asked us, his parents, to respect his conversion. The practice of this new religion went on for a few days. I was absolutely furious and wanted to go round to this man's house and give him a bollocking. Luckily, Kier soon gave up his religious observations and continued to watch TV and eat sweets in his spare time, as he had done formerly. Now I ask him why he converted, and he tells me he wanted to be like the other kids in his class. He didn't want to feel left out. I tell him there's nothing bad about feeling left out; in fact it could be a luxury, a pleasure and a form of self-determination that one might relish.

Sachin, Kier and I, in the sunshine, cross the Green and go back on to the Shepherd's Bush Road. It has been a lovely day.

23/12/2023

It is six in the morning and nearly Christmas when the strangers start to file into my house. I am lying on my front and taking a shit. A Brazilian woman, a Spanish woman, two Africans and an Italian have all come to either witness or help with what is kindly known as my care. As they stare at my arse, I feel no embarrassment, only a faint annoyance; this has become my fate and my life. Without all these people I couldn't function. Soon after, some of them leave and others remain to discuss my upkeep and the equipment I will need to get me out of bed and into the world each day.

Now, I spend my entire time in my kitchen and living room. It is a small area compared to the hospital, where I could zip about the corridors, the day room, the garden and the various pods. In my house I am more restricted. At least, as people say, I am home. But I am embarrassed, if not a little humiliated, when I see people I vaguely recognize and notice how they take me in, with sympathy or pity. I wonder what is going through their mind.

Every afternoon, for lack of other diversions, Isabella and I go to Tesco. It is something I look forward to, but the journey in a wheelchair is painful. Sometimes on the pavement there are obstructions: dumped mattresses or furniture that are impossible to pass. Not far from the entrance to Tesco, I notice a long-bearded enemy of mine from the 1970s, someone who always provoked me and who I looked down on. I see him waiting by the side of the road watching me as I go past. I try to ignore him, but he comes out and stands in front of me, saying, 'Hello, hello, hello,' so that I have to acknowledge him. He looks fit and reasonably well, while clearly I've been defeated. I never wanted to look weak in front of this man.

At Tesco, I enjoy whizzing about the aisles, and I am having to get used to what I call this 'dog's-eye view of the world' where I am at a lower level than everyone else. I find it odd that many people do not get out of the way when they see me coming at them. In fact they expect you to drive around them, as if you are the inconvenience. We buy Linda McCartney vegetarian sausages and what Isabella refers to as 'bak-ed beans' so that I may have my favourite meal. Isabella likes to rhyme 'bak-ed' with naked. That would make more sense, she argues plausibly.

In my kitchen, Isabella prepares food, cooks, washes up, and empties the bins. She has to do most of the housework while I can only look on or encourage her. The workload is uneven, and I am devastated by the level of responsibility she now has. My contribution is zilch. But I do not want to feel that I am a burden to her. Unfortunately, at the moment, there is no way around this. She cannot find time to do her job as a publicist for books and festivals in Italy. No one here would say that I am a liability, but certainly I feel that I am at least an impediment. Kier claims I never did so much around the house anyway, but I always did my best to help keep the place tidy and clean. Isabella and I discuss this issue and she always maintains her temper but I know it is draining for her to be kept from her work by my needs.

I am reminded of my situation as a child when both my parents were either depressed or in despair, and I would move between them, attempting to find conversation which would cheer them up. I had certain triggers that would do the trick, but not much worked with my mother. She would ignore me. With my father, I'd go into his bedroom, where he might be arranging his shirts or cleaning his shoes, and I'd start talking about writing or sports, subjects I knew would enliven him.

To a certain extent I have been doing this since, but now more than ever, because I have to keep those around me on my side; I cannot alienate them, I need them too much.

Christmas has been a worry for a while, as Isabella and I want to go to Tracey's to spend it with her and the family. The issue is whether I will be able to get into her house because there are two entrances, one into the basement and one above the front steps. We decide in the end, after much toing and froing, that I will be taken in a manual wheelchair to the bottom of the stairs, and Sachin and Carlo, who are quite strong, will carry me up and into the house.

To our surprise, it works well and is over quickly. Once inside, they move me into an armchair, which is the first time I have sat in anything but a wheelchair or hospital bed for a year. Tracey has brought the tables from the dining room up into the living room where we will have our lunch. We are all together: Carlo, Sachin, his girlfriend and her father, my carer, Isabella, and Cairo who sits under the table chewing Christmas paper. I am quieter than I used to be, I don't have much to say, but I am pleased and relieved to be here after so long away. We open our presents and Isabella reminds me that I have failed to get her anything. I know I should have sent one of the boys to Westfield. This is a terrible and guilt-inducing omission. She says that earlier in the month she hinted there was something she wanted, but I either failed to hear it, or failed to act on it.

Throughout the day, as the festivities continue, I am aware that it is more or less exactly a year since my accident. As anyone would, I relive the last moments of my ordinary life: travelling to Rome, having dinner with Isabella's family, working at her table together, and the next day going for a walk in the Villa Borghese before my blood pressure dropped, I fell on my head and was altered forever. How innocent we must seem when we don't know our fate. A man walking unknowingly into a disaster.

We are in constant development, never the same as yesterday. All the time we are changing, there is no going back. My world has taken a zig where previously it zagged; it has been smashed, remade and altered, and there is nothing I can do about it. But I will not go under; I will make something of this.

26/12/2023

Acknowledgements

During my year in hospital, many people supported me: friends and family, as well as doctors, nurses and other medical staff. I would like to thank them for all they did; without their dedication, this book would never have made it to the page.

Ceaselessly devoted and patient, much to my surprise, were my family: Isabella d'Amico, Carlo Kureishi, Sachin Kureishi, Kier Kureishi and Tracey Scoffield.

Friends:
Rachel Alexander
Michael Aminian
Charlotte Andrews
Lisa Appignanesi
Paolo Berro, Edoardo Arnello, Simone
    Scarzella and the AccessiWay Team
Giovanna Borsellino
Nicola Bottioni

Acknowledgements

Rosie Boycott
Virginia Brand and Charles Brand
Sonia Canfora
Mary Cannam
Julia Carruthers
Nanà Cecchi
Benedetta Craveri
Alessandro D'Alatri (Maestro)
Margherita d'Amico
Masolino d'Amico
Daniel Day-Lewis
Ashley Edwards
Richard Eyre
Jane Finlay
Nikolai Foster
Stephen Frears and Carolyn Hart
Steven Gale
David Gilmour and Polly Samson
David Goatley
David Gothard
Vivienne Guinness
Nigella Lawson
Darian Leader
Kevin Loader
Robert McCrum
Caroline Michel
Stephanie Morgan
Keith Munro

Serena Nono
Silvia Nono
Susie Orbach
Carlo Picozza
Rachel Purnell
Ruvani Ranasinha
Giacomo Regazzoni
Clare Reihill
Emma Rice
Ruth Rogers
Salman Rushdie and Rachel Eliza Griffiths
Kathy Sale
Samreen Shah
Richard Sharp
Paul Smith
Zadie Smith
Aurélia Thiérrée
Jeremy Thomas and Ludovica Barassi
Susie Thomas
Stewart Wallace
Tom Wilcox
Nigel Williams and Suzan Harrison
Nicholas Wright
Alan Yentob and Philippa Walker
Slavoj Žižek

I spent a year in several hospitals. I would like
to thank the teams who took care of me:

Policlinico Universitario Agostino Gemelli in
    Rome
Prof. Massimo Antonelli
Dr Nicola Cerbino
Prof. Alessandro Olivi
Dr Filippo Maria Polli

Fondazione Santa Lucia IRCCS in Rome
Dr Luca Battistini
Dr Lina Di Lucente
Fabio Marri
Dr Antonino Salvia
Dr Giorgio Scivoletto
Giada Serratore

The Charing Cross Neurological Rehabilitation
    Unit
Dr Meena Nayar and colleagues

The Royal National Orthopaedic Hospital at
    Stanmore
Nicki Ferguson
Dr Jan Gawronski
Dale Guthrie
Joseph (Joe) Steel
and the whole team

Andrew Kell and the team at Aspire, a charity that helps people with spinal injuries.

Thank you to the Paragon team and to my current carers:

Rosana Candia Barbosa
Blandine Vadjemia
Elisabeth (Lisa) Fabiam

And my thanks to those who worked on this book: Simon Prosser at Hamish Hamilton, Sarah Chalfant at the Wylie Agency and in particular Carlo Kureishi, my right hand.

A special mention to my dear friend Caroline Michel for her hard work, kindness and generosity.

Last but not least, I am grateful to the Substack community for their support, and also to the Royal Literary Fund, particularly Edward Kemp, for their continuing work.

I will be very grateful to anyone who is able to support me with my ongoing care.

hanifkureishi.org